AF651739

Hanuman Chalisa

By Goswami Tulsidas

Presented by : Divinebharat

Copyright © 2025 divinebharat
All rights reserved.
For permission
Contact:
info.divinebharat@gmail.com
ISBN: 978-93-343-6248-0

https://www.divinebharat.co

Table of Contents

HANUMAN CHALISA

|| Doha ||

Shri Guru Charan Saroj Raj,
Nija Manu Mukura Sudhari |

Baranau Raghuvar Bimal Jasu,
Jo Dayaku Phala Chari ||

Budheeheen Tanu Jannike,
Sumiro Pavan Kumara |

Bal Buddhi Vidya Dehoo Mohee,
Harahu Kalesh Vikaar ||

|| Chaupai ||

Jai Hanuman Gyan Gun Sagar
| Jai Kapis Tihun Lok Ujagar ||
Ram Doot Atulit Bal Dhama |
Anjani Putra Pavan Sut Nama ||
Mahabir Vikram Bajrangi |
Kumati Nivar Sumati Ke Sangi ||
Kanchan Varan Viraj Subesa |
Kanan Kundal Kunchit Kesha || 4

Hath Vajra Aur Dhwaja Viraje |
Kaandhe Moonj Janeu Saaje ||
Sankar Suvan Kesri Nandan |
Tej Prataap Maha Jag Vandan ||
Vidyavaan Guni Ati Chatur |
Ram Kaj Karibe Ko Aatur ||
Prabhu Charitra Sunibe Ko Rasiya |
Ram Lakhan Sita Man Basiya || 8

Sukshma Roop Dhari Siyahi Dikhava |
Vikat Roop Dhari Lank Jalava ||
Bhim Roop Dhari Asur Sanhare |
Ramachandra Ke Kaj Sanvare ||
Laye Sanjivan Lakhan Jiyaye |
Shri Raghuvir Harashi Ur. Laye ||
Raghupati Kinhi Bahut Badai |
Tum Mama Priya Bharat-Hi-Sam
Bhai ||12

Sahas Badan Tumharo Yash Gaave |
As Kahi Shripati Kanth Lagaave ||
Sankadhik Brahmaadi Muneesa |
Narad Sarad Sahit Aheesa ||
Jam Kuber Dikpaal Jahan Te |
Kavi Kovid Kahi Sake Kahan Te ||
Tum Upkar Sugreevahin Keenha |
Ram Milaye Rajpad Deenha || 16

Tumhro Mantra Vibheeshan Maana |
Lankeshwar Bhaye Sab Jag Jana ||
Jug Sahasra Yojan Par Bhanu |
Leelyo Tahi Madhur Phal Janu ||
Prabhu Mudrika Meli Mukh Mahee |
Jaladhi Langhi Gaye Achraj Nahee ||
Durgam Kaj Jagat Ke Jete |
Sugam Anugraha Tumhre Tete || 20

Ram Duwaare Tum Rakhvare |
Hot Na Agya Binu Paisare ||
Sab Sukh Lahai Tumhari Sarna |
Tum Rakshak Kahu Ko Darna ||
Aapan Tej Samharo Aapai |
Teenon Lok Hank Te Kanpai ||
Bhoot Pisaach Nikat Nahin Aavai |
Mahavir Jab Naam Sunavai || 24

Nase Rog Harae Sab Peera |
Japat Nirantar Hanumat Beera ||
Sankat te Hanuman Chhudavai |
Man Kram Vachan Dhyan Jo Lavai ||
Sab Par Ram Tapasvee Raja |
Tin Ke Kaj Sakal Tum Saja ||
Aur Manorath Jo Koi Lavai |
Soi Amit Jeevan Phal Pavai || 28

Charon Jug Partap Tumhara |
Hai Parsiddh Jagat Ujiyara ||
Sadhu Sant Ke Tum Rakhware |
Asur Nikandan Ram Dulare ||
Ashta Siddhi Nav Nidhi Ke Data |
As Var Deen Janki Mata ||
Ram Rasayan Tumhare Pasa |
Sada Raho Raghupati Ke Dasa || 32

Tumhare Bhajan Ram Ko Pavai |
Janam Janam Ke Dukh Bisraavai ||
Antkaal Raghuvar Pur Jayee |
Jahan Janam Hari Bhakt Kahayee ||
Aur Devta Chitt Na Dharahin |
Hanumat Sei Sarv Sukh Karahin ||
Sankat Kate Mite Sab Peera |
Jo Sumirai Hanumat Balbeera || 36

Jai Jai Jai Hanuman Gosain |
Kripa Karahun Gurudev Ki Nayin ||
Jo Shat Bar Path Kare Koi |
Chhutahin Bandi Maha Sukh Hoi ||
Jo Yeh Padhe Hanuman Chalisa |
Hoye Siddhi Saakhi Gaureesa ||
Tulsidas Sada Hari Chera |
Keejai Nath Hriday Mahn Dera || 40

|| Doha ||

Pavan Tanay Sankat Harana,
Mangala Murati Roop |
Ram Lakhan Sita Sahita,
Hriday Basahu Soor Bhoop ||

Sankat Mochan Hanuman Ashtak

Baal samai ravi bhakshi liyo tab,
teenahu loka bhayo andhiyaro ।
Taahi so traas bhayo jag ko,
yah sankat kaahu so jaat na taaro ।
Dewan aani kari bintee tab,
chaadhi diyo ravi kasht niwaaro ।
Ko nahin jaanat hai jag mein kapi,
sankat mochan naam tihaaro ॥1॥

Baali ki traas kapees basai giri,
jaat mahaaprabhu panth nihaaro ।
Chowki mahaa muni saap diyo tab,
chahiy kaun bichaar bichaaro ।
Kai dwij roop liwaay mahaa prabhu,
so tum daas ke sok niwaaro ।
Ko nahin jaanat hai jag mein kapi,
sankat mochan naam tiharo ॥2॥

Angad ke sang lain gaye siya,
khoj kapees yah baain uchaaro I
jeevat na bachihau hum son ju,
bina sudhi laay ehaan pagu dhaaro I
Heyri thake tatt sindhu sabaai tab,
laay siya-sudhi praan ubaaro I
Ko nahin jaanat hai jag mein kapi,
sankat mochan naam tiharo II3II

Raavan traas dayee siya ko sab,
raakshashi so kahi sok nivaaro I
Taahi samay hanuman mahaprabhu,
Jaay mahaa rajneechar maaro I
Chaahat seeya asoka so aagi su,
dai prabhu mudrika soka nivaaro I
Ko nahin jaanat hai jag mein kapi,
sankat mochan naam tiharo II4II

Baan lagyo ur lakshiman ke tab,
praan taje sut raavan maaro I
Lai griha baidya sushen samet,
tabai giri dron su beer upaaro I
Aani sajeewan hath dayee taba,
lakshiman ke tum praan ubaaro I
Ko nahin jaanat hai jag mein kapi,
sankat mochan naam tiharo II5II

Raavan yudh ajaan kiyo tab,
naag ki phaas sabhi sir daaro ।
Sri Raghunath samet sabai dal,
moh bhayo yah sankat bhaaro ।
Aani khagesh tabai hanumaan ju,
bandhan kaati sutraas nivaaro ।
Ko nahin jaanat hai jag mein kapi,
sankat mochan naam tiharo ॥6॥

Bandhu samet jabai ahiraavan,
lai raghunath pataal sidhaaro ।
Devhi puji bhalee vidhi so bali,
deu sabai mili mantra vichaaro ।
Jaay sahaay bhayo tab hi,
ahiraavan sainya samet sanhaaro ।
Ko nahin jaanat hai jag mein kapi,
sankat mochan naam tiharo ॥7॥

Kaaj kiye barh dewan kei tum,
beer mahaaprabhu dekhi bichaaro ।
Kaun so sankat mohin gareeb ko,
jo tumso nahin jaat hai taaro ।
Begi haro hanumaan mahaprabhu,
jo kuch sankat hoya hamaaro ।
Ko nahin jaanat hai jag mein kapi,
sankat mochan naam tiharo ॥8॥

॥ Doha ॥

Laal deh laalee lase,
aru dhari laal langoor ।
Bajra deh daanavdalan,
jai jai jai kapi soor ॥

॥ Iti sankatmochan Hanumanastak sampurna ॥

Shri Hanumat Stavan

Pranavau Pavan Kumar
khal ban paavak gyaan ghan,
Jaasu hriday aagaar basahi
Ram sar chaap dhar. ||1||

Atulit bal dhaamam
hem shailaabh deham,
Danuj van krishaanum
gyaaninaam agraganyam. ||2||

Sakal gun nidhaanam
vaanaraanaam dheesham,
Raghupati priya bhaktam
Vaatjaatam namaami. ||3||

Goshpadeekrit vaareesham
mashakeekrit raakshasam,
Ramayan mahamala ratnam
vande Anilaatmajam. ||4||

Anjananandanam veeram
Janaki shokanashanam,
Kapeesham aksha hantaaram
vande Lanka bhayankaram. ||5||

**Mahavyaakaranambhodhi
manthamaanasa mandaram,
Kavayantam Ramakeertyaa
Hanumantam upaasmahe. ||6||**

**Ullanghya sindhoh salilam salilam,
Yah shoka vahnim Janakaatmajaayah.
Aadaaya tenaiva dadaaha Lankam,
Namaami tam pranjaliraanjaneyam.
||7||**

**Manojavam marutatulya vegam,
Jitendriyam buddhimataam
varishtham,
Vaatatmajam vaanarayuthmukhyam,
Shree Ramdootam sharanam
prapadye. ||8||**

**Anjaneyam ati paatalaananam,
Kanchanaadrikamaniya vigraham,
Paarijaatataru moola vaasinam,
Bhaavayaami Pavamana nandanam.
||9||**

Yatra yatra Raghunath keertanam,
Tatra tatra kritamastaka anjalim,
Vaashpa vaari paripurna lochanam,
Maarutim namata raakshasaantakam.
||10||

Shri Hanuman Ji Ki Aarti

Aarti keeje Hanumaan lalaa kee,
Dusht dalan Raghunaath kalaa kee.

Jaake bal se Girivar kaanpe,
Rog dosh jaake nikat na jhaanke.1
Anjani putra mahaabaldaayi,
Santaan ke prabhu sadaa sahaayi.2
Dev bira Raghunaath pathaaye,
Lanka jaari Siya sudhi laaye.3
Lanka so kot samudra si khaai,
Jaat Pavan sut baar na laayi.4
Lanka jaari asur sanhaare,
Siyaram ji ke kaaj sanvaare.5
Lakshman moorchhit pare sakaare,
Aani Sanjeevan praan ubaare.6
Paithi Pataal tori Jam-kaare,
Ahiraavan ki bhujaa ukhaade.7
Baayein bhujaa asur dal maare,
Daahine bhujaa santjan taare.8
Sur-nar-muni jan Aarti utaare,
Jai Jai Jai Hanumaan uchaare.9
Kanchan thaar kapoor lau chhaayi,
Aarti karat Anjanaa maai.10
Lanka vidhvans keenh Raghuraai,
Tulsidaas prabhu keerti gaai.11
Jo Hanumaan ji ki Aarti gaave,
Basi Baikunth param pad paave.12

Sri Ram Vandana

Aapdaam-apahartaaram
daataaram sarva-sampadaam,
Lokaabhiramam Shri-Raamam
bhooyo bhooyo namaamyaham.

Raamaaya Raamabhadraaya
Raamachandraaya maanase,
Raghunaathaaya naathaaya
Seetaayaah pataye namah.

Neelaambuja-shyaamala-
komalaangam,
Seeta-samaaropita-
vaama-bhaagam,
Paanau mahaasaayaka-
chaaru-chaapam,
Namaami Raamam
Raghuvamsanaatham.

|| Iti Shri Ram Vandana ||

Sri Ram Stuti

Shri Raamachandra
kripaalu bhajuman,
Haran bhavabhay daarunam.
Nav kanj lochan kanj mukh,
Kar kanj pad kanjaarunam. ||1||
Kandarp aganit amit chhavi,
Nav neel neerad sundaram.
Patpeet maanahu tadit ruchi shuchi,
Nomi Janak sutaavaram. ||2||
Bhaju deenbandhu dinesh daanav,
Daitya vansh nikandanam.
Raghunand aanand kand Kaushal,
Chand Dasharath nandanam. ||3||
Shir mukut kundal tilak,
Chaaru udaaru ang vibhooshanam.
Aajaanu bhuj shar chaap dhar,
Sangraam jit Khar-dooshanam. ||4||
Iti vadati Tulsidaas Shankar,
Shesh muni man ranjanam.
Mam hriday kanj nivaas kuru,
Kaamadi khaldal ganjanam. ||5||
Man jaahi raachyo milahi so,
Var sahaj sundar saanwaro.
Karuna nidhaan sujaan sheel,
Sneh jaanat Raavaro. ||6||
Ehi bhaanti Gauri asees sun,
Siy sahit hiya harshit ali.
Tulsi Bhavaanihi pooji puni-puni,
Mudit man mandir chali. ||7||

|| Soratha ||

Jaani Gauri anukool Siy,
Hiya harashu na jaai kahi.
Manjul mangal mool baam,
Ang pharakan lage.

Shri Ramavatar Stotra

Bhaye pragat kripala
deen dayaala Kausalya hitakaari,
Harshit meh-taari muni man haari
adbhut roop bichaari.
Lochan abhirama tanu
ghanasyaama nij aayudh bhuja chaari,
Bhushan banmaala nayan bisala
sobha sindhu kharaari. ||1||

Kah dui kar jori astuti tori
kehi bidhi karau ananta,
Maayaa gun gyaanateet amaanaa
ved puraan bhananta.
Karuna sukh saagar sab gun
aagar jehi gaavahi shruti santa,
So mam hit laagi jan anuraagi
bhayau pragat Shri Kanta. ||2||

Brahmaand nikaaya nirmit maayaa
rom rom prati ved kahay,
Mam ur so baasi yah upahaasi
sunat dheer mati thir na rahay.
Up-ja jab gyaana Prabhu musukaana
charit bahut bidhi keenh chahay,
Kahi katha suhaayi maat bujhaayi
jehi prakaar sut prem lahay4. ||3||

Maataa puni boli so mati
doli tajahu taat yah roopa,
Keejai sisulila ati priyasiila
yah sukh param anoopa.
Suni bachan sujaana rodana
thaana hoi baalak Surabhoopa,
Yah charit je gaavahi haripad
paavahi te na parahi bhavakoopa. ||4||

|| Doha ||

Vipra dhenu sur sant hit,
leenhu manuj avatar,
Nij ichchha nirmit tanu,
maayoun gun goopaar.

Shiv Panchakshar Stotra

Naagendra-haaraaya trilochanaaya
Bhasmaang-raagaaya Maheshwaraaya
Nityaaya shuddhaaya digambaraaya
Tasmai N-kaaraaya namah Shivaaya
Mandaakinee-salila-chandana-
charchitaaya
Nandeeshwara-pramatha-naatha-
Maheshwaraaya
Mandaar-pushpa-bahu-pushpa-
supoojitaaya
Tasmai M-kaaraaya namah Shivaaya
Shivaaya Gauri-vadanaabja-vrinda
Suuryaaya dakshaadhvara-naashakaaya
Shree-neelakanthaaya vrishadhvajaaya
Tasmai Shi-kaaraaya namah Shivaaya
Vashishtha-kumbhodbhava-gautama-arya
Muneendra-devaarchita-shekhaaraaya
Chandraarka-vaishwaanara-lochanaaya
Tasmai Va-kaaraaya namah Shivaaya
Yajna-swaroopaaya jataadharaaya
Pinaaka-hastaaya sanaatanaaya
Divyaaya devaaya digambaraaya
Tasmai Ya-kaaraaya namah Shivaaya

Phalasruti:

Panchaksharamidam punyam
yah pathet Shiva-sannidhau
Shivalokam-avaapnoti
Shivena saha modate

9 789334 362480

Printed at Repro India Ltd.

Thermo-Physical Properties of Rocks

Special Reference to Deccan Trap Basalts

Thermo-Physical Properties of Rocks

Special Reference to Deccan Trap Basalts

S.R. Sharma

Former Scientist

National Geophysical Research Institute, Hyderabad

ALLIED PUBLISHERS PVT. LTD.

New Delhi • Mumbai • Kolkata • Lucknow • Chennai
Nagpur • Bangalore • Hyderabad • Ahmedabad

ALLIED PUBLISHERS PRIVATE LIMITED

Regd. Off.: 15 J.N. Heredia Marg, Ballard Estate, **Mumbai**–400001
Ph.: 022-22626476 • E-mail: mumbai.books@alliedpublishers.com

1/13-14 Asaf Ali Road, **New Delhi**–110002
Ph.: 011-23239001 • E-mail: delhi.books@alliedpublishers.com

17 Chittaranjan Avenue, **Kolkata**–700072
Ph.: 033-22129618 • E-mail: cal.books@alliedpublishers.com

751 Anna Salai, **Chennai**–600002
Ph.: 044-28523938 • E-mail: chennai.books@alliedpublishers.com

5th Main Road, Gandhinagar, **Bangalore**–560009
Ph.: 080-22262081 • E-mail: bngl.books@alliedpublishers.com

3-2-844/6 & 7 Kachiguda Station Road, **Hyderabad**–500027
Ph.: 040-24619079 • E-mail: hyd.books@alliedpublishers.com

60 Shiv Sunder Apartments (Ground Floor), Central Bazar Road,
Bajaj Nagar, **Nagpur**–440010

F-1 Sun House (First Floor), C.G. Road, Navrangpura,
Ellisbridge P.O., **Ahmedabad**–380006
Ph.: 079-26465916 • E-mail: ahmbd.books@alliedpublishers.com

Khasra No. 168, Plot No. 12-A, Opp. Wisdom Academy School,
Kamta, Surendra Nagar, **Lucknow**–227105
Ph.: 09335202549 • E-mail: lko.books@alliedpublishers.com

Website: www.alliedpublishers.com

© 2015, Author

No part of the material protected by this copyright notice may be reproduced or utilized in any form or by any means, electronic or mechanical including photocopying, recording or by any information storage and retrieval system, without prior written permission from the copyright owners.

ISBN: 978-81-8424-979-8

Published by Sunil Sachdev and printed
by Ravi Sachdev at Allied Publishers Pvt. Ltd.
(Printing Division), A-104 Mayapuri Phase II, New Delhi-110064

Foreword

Over the years literature, both experimental data of properties of rocks and their application in interpreting various Geo-Phenomena and evaluating various earth's resources, has grown and is growing. The Present Book **"Thermo-Physical Properties of Rocks: Special Reference to Deccan Trap Basalts"** is first of its kind in India. It fills a great gap and necessity by providing at one place, not only a compilation of the different types of thermos-physical and other properties of rocks and basalts from the Deccan trap region of India in particular, but also description of methods of measurements and basic theory. Dr. S.R. Sharma has done a wonderful job with great insight. The benefit of the data which was available in a scattered way till now, is now extended to all who need this important data and knowledge for their work.

I am happy to forward this Book, which would be valuable and useful to Students, Professionals, in various fields of applications and researchers in the discipline of earth's science and its resources.

Dr. Mohan L. Gupta
Geothermal Consultant
Formerly with CSIR – National Geophysical Research Institute, Hyderabad

Preface

The interpretation of geophysical data in exploration geophysics, well logging, engineering, mining and environmental geophysics requires knowledge and correlation of Thermo-physical properties on rocks and minerals at NTP and high pressure-temperature conditions. Thermo-physical properties include thermal conductivity, thermal diffusivity, heat capacity, pore space properties, density, electrical properties, magnetic properties, seismic/elastic properties and nuclear properties, etc. Knowledge of these properties provide the basis for the interpretation of the geophysical measurements of seismic velocities, electrical conductivity, and temperature gradients in terms of unknown quantities, such as mineralogical, chemical composition, temperature, heat flow, and fluid content, etc., at depth in the earth and moon. Also, their co-relationship is useful to determine the unknown property if one entity is known. Thus it becomes important to suggest the possible explanation of the geophysical/geological anomalies observed in field investigations and other tectonic processes in the earth's crust/mantle, prospecting for ground water, hydrocarbon and geothermal resources, etc.

Systematic measurements and compilation of the data on all the properties on rocks/minerals and their co-relations to understand more and more about the geological/geophysical problems and governing process in the earth's are ongoing programs in almost all the developing countries. However, systematic compilation of published and unpublished data in the form of a book on thermo-physical and other properties of rocks are very rare or rather not done in India. These data on rocks, basalts from Deccan trap regions and the correlations among the various properties will be very useful to understand the problems related to source magma composition, crystallization conditions, depth of source magma and governing processes in the earth crust in earthquake regions of Deccan Traps.

With this as a backdrop, a systematic compilation of published and unpublished data on thermo-physical properties on rocks and basalts from Deccan Traps regions has been done. This book is designed to provide a comprehensive introduction to the rocks and thermo-physical properties of rocks and minerals at NTP and elevated temperature and pressure. The chapters covered in this book include introduction, thermal properties, density-porosity-permeability, electrical properties, seismic properties, magnetic properties and natural radioactivity of crust-mantle rocks and minerals with special reference to Deccan Basalts. The introduction covers the nature of the earth's crust, mantle and core, various types of rocks, their petrology and processes involved in their formation. It also includes the nature of the Deccan Traps and the processes involved in its formation, etc. in brief. Other chapters deal with the basics of relevant properties, units, measurement techniques, co-relation with other geophysical parameters and applications.

Keeping in view, my 34 years research experience in the field of geophysics in National Geophysical Research Institute, Hyderabad which is one of the renowned research organizations of the world in the field of Geosciences, this book is written for the benefit of the students, research scholars and scientists working in the field of earth sciences.

S.R. Sharma

Former Scientist-NGRI, 8-7, Hema Nagar Colony,
Road-10, Plot-343, Uppal Post, Hyderabad–500 039 (AP)

Acknowledgements

My thanks and appreciation to Dr. M.L. Gupta, my mentor, and Dr. P.S. Mahesh, my teacher, to motivate and guide me to write this book and for persevering with me as my advisor throughout the time it took me to complete. I must acknowledge as well the many friends, colleagues who assisted, advised, and supported my work and writing efforts. I need to express my gratitude and deep appreciation, especially to Dr. V.K. Rao, Dr. D.M. Mall, Dr. G.V.S.P. Rao, Mr. P.N. Sharma and Mr. Anish Kumar of National Geophysical Research Institute (NGRI), Hyderabad. I am also grateful for the support, advice and valuable discussions with my senior colleagues Dr. H.K. Gupta, Dr. V.P. Dimri, Dr. U. Raval and Dr. D.C. Mishra of NGRI for their encouragement and consistent advice. I also thank Dr. Y.J. Bhaskar Rao, Director, NGRI for his support and invaluable advice and also allowing me to avail the library facilities. I acknowledge the support of library staff for their kind help. I have great appreciation to reviewers for their critical comments which helped me to improve the project. Thanks also to Mr. Ajay Ram Chandar, MCA for his help in the preparation of this book, and the publisher to publish it.

In addition, I would like to acknowledge the Department of Science and Technology, Ministry of Science and Technology, New Delhi for providing the financial support for the project "Thermo-Physical Properties of Rocks: Special Reference to

Deccan Trap Basalts" and the Vichitra Maitreyee Samman (VMS), a Non-Governmental Organization, New Delhi being the via media for the financial support. I am also grateful to Vichitra Maitreyee Samman (VMS) for their administrative and financial support.

I also acknowledge the support of my family members for their support and being my strength. Finally, I dedicate this book to the memory of my wife, Saroj Devi Sharma in gratitude for perfect companionship and help in all things. Her infallible strength and faith during the last year of her life gave me a new appreciation for the meaning and importance of life.

(S.R. Sharma)

Contents

CHAPTER I Introduction

Our planet Earth is a very complex body, of which a small part is available to us for direct observations. In order to investigate the physical state of its deep interior, experiments have to be performed under physical conditions similar to those occur at depth and also on possible rocks which can be expected in the region of interest. Various physical and chemical methods such as electrical, magnetic, thermal, gravity, seismic, radioactivity, isotopic, geochemical, etc. are used for the exploration and assessment of its numerous natural resources on which prosperity and many of the daily requirements of the mankind depend today.

A knowledge of the physical properties such as electrical conductivity, acoustic velocities, thermal, magnetic and elastic properties, etc. of the near surface rocks, is therefore, of immense use in interpretation of field results. Knowledge of the physical properties provides also the basis for the interpretation of the geophysical measurements of seismic velocities, electrical conductivity, and temperature gradients in terms of unknown quantities, such as mineralogical, chemical composition, temperature, heat flow, and fluid content, etc., at depth in the earth and moon.

Thermo-physical properties like density, porosity, specific heat, thermal diffusivity, thermal conductivity, magnetic suscepti-bility and magnetic intensity of crust/mantle rocks and their correlation are very important to understand the anomalies observed in geological/geophysical field investigations and in the interpretation of geophysical data in exploration geophysics, well logging, engineering, mining and environmental geophysics. Physical properties are a "key" for combined interpretation techniques.

The interpretation of geophysical data in exploration geophysics, well logging, engineering, mining and environmental geophysics requires knowledge of the physical properties of the rocks and their correlation. Thermo-physical properties are thermal conductivity, thermal diffusivity, heat capacity, pore space properties, density, electrical properties, magnetic properties, seismic/elastic properties and nuclear properties, etc. Their inter co-relationship is useful to determine the unknown property if one is known and thereby becomes important to suggest the possible explanation of the geophysical/geological anomalies observed in field investigations.

Magnetic properties on lower crustal rocks are very useful to understand the magnetic nature of crust and to explain the anomalies regarding magnetic crust observed by MAGSAT data and heat flow studies. Likewise electrical resistivity of rocks is important for geophysical prospecting for mineral/water/hydrocarbons/geothermal resources. Variation of electrical conductivity at elevated temperatures is very helpful to interpret the subsurface electrical conductivity structure using geo-electric/electromagnetic methods. Thermal diffusivity measurements at room temperature and high temperatures are useful to understand the thermal history of the region and hydrocarbon fields. Radioactive heat generation in rocks is an important constituent of the heat flow studies and radioactive elements prospecting and to explain the anomalies observed in heat flow in order to understand the thermal structure of the earth's interior.

Rocks occur in the earth's interior as interrelated bodies of different origin, geometry, size, composition, structure, etc. The interpretation of geophysical/Geological data to understand the processes in the earth's interior needs the knowledge of the rock properties and their correlation. Growing interest in rock physics results from the need to extend more information from geophysical measurements concerning the accuracy, reliability and validity of the results. Rock physics is an integrating part of this process, because it couples and connects the different disciplines. One must have knowledge of different types of thermo-physical properties, and petrochemical characteristics.

With this in backdrop, it is proposed to compile different types of thermo-physical and other properties on rocks and basalts from the Deccan trap region. This region, covering an exposed area of about 0.5 million sq. km. consists of large number of lava flows of different origin, composition, structure, etc. Latur, Bhuj, and Jabalpur areas of Deccan Trap region are earthquake affected areas where deep crustal earthquakes occurred in the past. Detailed geophysical/geological field investigations were carried out and are in the process in these areas. But systematic studies of the thermo-physical and radioactive properties on the rocks from these areas were not carried out so far. However, some thermo-physical properties on rocks from these areas have been measured and published as and when necessary. These properties and their co-relation found very useful to interpret the mineral composition, presence of ferromagnetic minerals, comparative depths of source magma and crystallization conditions of the magma flows.

Using MAGSAT data, Curie depth beneath Indian shield has been suggested from 30–43 km, considering the temperature 550°C as the demagnetization temperature of magnetite. Curie depth estimated using heat flow data varies from 20 to 54 km beneath Indian Shield. Discrepancies in the estimation of magnetic crust using the MAGSAT data and heat flow data indicate the variation in magnetic minerals in lower crust (Sharma *et al.*, 2005). To understand the magnetic composition variation in the lower crust beneath Indian Shield it will be very useful to compile the data on thermo-physical and other properties of rocks and Deccan Basalts.

1.1 Earth Structure

The earth consists of several layers. The three main layers are the core, the mantle and the crust. The core is the inner part of the earth, the crust is the outer part and between them is the mantle Figure 1.1. The earth is surrounded by the atmosphere. Till this moment it hasn't been possible to take a look inside the earth because the current technology doesn't allow it. Therefore all kinds of research had to be done to find out; out of which material the earth consists, what different layers there are and which influence those have (had) on the earth's surface.

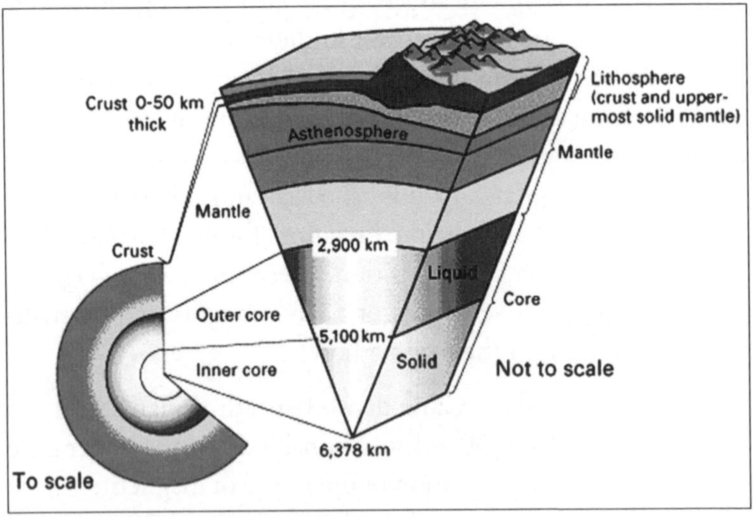

Fig. 1.1: Structure of the Earth

1.1.1 *Core*

The inner part of the earth is the core. This part of the earth is about 2,900 km below the earth's surface. The core is a dense ball of the elements iron and nickel. It is divided into two layers, the inner core and the outer core. The inner core—the centre of earth—is solid and about 1,250 km thick. The outer core is so hot that the metal is always molten, but the inner core pressures are so great that it cannot melt, even though temperatures there reach ~5000°C. The outer core is about 2,200 km thick. Because the earth rotates, the outer core spins around the inner core and that causes the earth's magnetism.

1.1.2 *Mantle*

The Earth's mantle is a ~2,900 km thick shell of compressed and heated rock, beginning below the Earth's crust, which extends 5 km below the ocean floor and 30 to 50 km below the continents. The Earth's mantle makes up 70% of Earth's volume, in comparison to the Earth's crust which makes up less than 1% of the total. The crust and mantle are separated by a transition area called the Mohorovičić) discontinuity (the "Moho") where a certain type of seismic wave quickly speeds up when transiting through. Below the mantle are the outer core and inner core of the Earth, making up about 29% of the Earth's volume, and composed primarily of molten (outer core) or solid (inner core) iron and nickel. The mantle is divided into sections based upon results from seismology. These layers are 1) the upper mantle (starting at the Moho, downward to 410 km), the transition zone (410–660 km), and 2) the lower mantle (660–2891 km), and in the bottom of the latter region there is the anomalous D" layer with a variable thickness (on average ~200 km thick). The upper mantle has a low density relative to the rest of the mantle, and flows fluidly, like a plastic because of the increasing temperature and pressures as you descend into the Earth.

1.1.3 *Crust*

The crust lies above the mantle and is the earth's hard outer shell, the surface on which we are living. In relation with the other layers the crust is much thinner. It floats upon the softer, denser mantle. The crust is made up of solid material but this material is not everywhere the same. There is an Oceanic crust and a Continental crust. The first one is about 6–11 km thick and consists of heavy rocks, like basalt. The Continental crust is thicker than the Oceanic crust, about 30–50 km thick. It consists of different types of rocks which are formed from the solidification magma which comes at the surface due to different geological/geophysical/thermal, etc. processes in the crust, mantle and core. Therefore, different processes occurred in the subsurface are reflected on the earth surface in the form of the changes in the properties of rocks.

Eight elements make up 99% (by weight) of the minerals that form solid earth. Weight and volume of the principal element in the earth crust (Foster, 1971) are shown in Table 1.1.

Table 1.1: Weight and Volume of the Principal Elements in the Earth's Crust

Element	*Weight %*	*Volume %*
Oxygen	46.4	94.05
Silicon	28.15	0.88
Aluminium	8.23	0.48
Iron	5.63	0.48
Calcium	4.15	1.19
Sodium	2.36	1.11
Magnesium	2.33	0.32
Potassium	2.09	1.49

Although the crust appears to be very heterogeneous with respect to minerals and rocks, most of it actually composed of combination of only eight elements with trace amounts of others. The estimated and calculated composition (weight %) of the earth crust, mantle and core is shown in Table 1.2 (Schon, 1996).

Table 1.2: The Composition (weight %) of the Earth's Crust, Mantle and Core

Element	*Crust*	*Mantle*	*Core*
O	47.25	43.7	–
si	30.54	22.5	–
Al	7.83	1.6	–
Fe	3.54	9.88	86.3
Ca	2.87	1.67	–
K	2.82	0.11	–
Na	2.45	0.84	–
Mg	1.39	18.8	–
Ti	0.47	0.08	–
P	0.08	0.14	–
Mn	0.07	0.33	–
Ni	0.0044	–	7.36
Co	0.0012	–	0.40
S	0.031	–	5.94
Total	**99.3466**	**99.65**	**100.0**

1.2 Rocks of the Earth

Rocks comprising the lithosphere have formed by interaction between matter and various form of energy-chiefly gravitational and thermal- over the 4.5 Ga history of the earth.

The wide range of rock forming geological processes and environmental conditions of temperature (T), Pressure (P) and the concentration of chemical species related to these complex interactions have created a wide spectrum of rock properties. Subsurface earth materials come on the surface due to various geological, geochemical and geothermal processes. On the basis of the formation, origin and character of rocks, Geologists and Petrologists have classified the rocks of the earth into three main groups vis., i) igneous rocks, ii) sedimentary rocks and iii) meta-morphic rocks as shown in Table 1.3. The main group of rocks are termed as igneous and sedimentary and their metamorphic equivalents. Igneous rocks are the product of crystallization of naturally occurring silicate melts where as sedimentary rocks result from the accumulation of material at the surface of the earth by various processes under the influence of agents such as wind, water, and ice. Metamorphic rocks result from recrystallization of igneous and sedimentary rocks at relatively high temperature and pressure (Carnichael, 1982).

1.2.1 *Igneous Rocks*

Igneous rocks are formed directly from the cooling of magma, the source of which is within the earth. Under favorable conditions, the molten material is forced upwards and erupted in the form of volcanoes. This is an exothermic process (it loses heat) and involves a phase change from the liquid to the solid state. The rocks which are formed by the cooling and solidification of magma under the influence of surrounding rocks at some depth below the surface are designated as intrusive or plutonic rocks. Extrusive or volcanic rocks are formed by the solidification of magma at the surface. Based upon composition and texture, the igneous rocks are given names as shown in Table 1.3.

Table 1.3: Igneous Rock Classifications

Rock Type	*Texture-ave. Size of Minerals*	*General Color and/or Composition – Miscellaneous Observations*	*Rock Name*
Igneous Rocks Interlocking homogenous crystalline texture – no preferred orientation to the mineral grains	Fine grained Extrusive, volcanic	Felsic – Light colored	Rhyolite
		Intermediate	Andesite
		Mafic – Dark colored	Basalt
	Medium grained Dikes, sills, etc.	Felsic – Light colored	–
		Intermediate	Dacite
		Mafic – Dark colored	Diabase
	Coarse grained Generally intrusive	Felsic – Light colored	Granite
		Intermediate	Diorite
		Mafic – Dark colored	Gabbro
		Ultramafic	Peridotite
	Glassy	Dark to black – felsic (does not follow normal color index)	Obsidian
	Frothy	Felsic – Light colored	Pumice
		Mafic – Dark colored	Scoria
Sedimentary Rocks Consolidated detrital clasts, chemical precipitates, and/or biological residue	Coarse Fragments	Rounded clasts	Conglomerate
		Angular clasts	Breccia
	Sand sized fragments	Clean quartz (w/feldspar?)	Sandstone
		Dirty w/rock fragments and clay	Graywacke
	Fine grained – cannot see individual clasts	Nonfoliated, "clay the size"	Siltstone
		Foliated, "clay the mineral"	Shale
	Chemical – fine grain	Soft – passes fizz test	Limestone
		Hard – fails fizz test	Chert
	Fossiliferous	Mostly shell fragments	Coquina
Metamorphic Rocks Interlocking non-homogenous crystalline texture – commonly with a preferred orientation to the mineral grains	FOLIATED: Very fine grained- no visible minerals	Dull – passes "tink test"	Slate
		Foliated, shiny due to increased size of micaceous minerals (almost see them)	Phyllite
	FOLIATED: Medium to coarse grain	Individual mineral grains visible. Major mineral(s) included as name modifiers	Schist (ex. Mica Schist)
	FOLIATED: Color banded	Alternating layers of light (felsic) and dark (mafic) minerals	Gneiss
	FOLIATED: Distinct layering – often highly folded and contorted	Alternating layers of felsic igneous rock (light) and mafic gneiss (dark)	Migmatite
	Non-foliated, with non-oriented grains	Soft – passes fizz test	Marble
		Hard – fails fizz test	Quartzite

1.2.1.1 *Plutonic Rocks*

Coarse grained rocks. Rocks are Gabbro, Diorite, Granodirite and Granite.

1.2.1.2 *Volcanic Rocks*

Basalt 48–52% Silica, temperature of the magma: 1160°C
Andesite 52–63% Silica
Dacite 63–68% Silica
Rhyolite—more than 68% Silica, Temperature of magma: 900°C
Temperature of the magma: 600–1160°C
Mobility decreases from Basalt to Rhyolite.

1.2.2 *Sedimentary Rocks*

These rocks are formed by the deposition of the weathered remains of other rocks at the Earth's surface and within bodies of water; by the deposition of the results of biogenic activity; and by precipitation from solution. Sedimentation is the collective name for processes that cause mineral and/or organic particles to settle and accumulate or minerals to precipitate from a solution. Particles that form a sedimentary rock by accumulating are called sediment. Before being deposited, sediment was formed by weathering and erosion in a source area, and then transported to the place of deposition by water, wind, ice, mass movement or glaciers. Sedimentary rocks include common types such as chalk, limestone, sandstone, and shale.

Sedimentary rocks contain important information about the history of the Earth. They contain fossils, the preserved remains of ancient plants and animals. The composition of sediments provides us with clues as to the original rock. Differences between successive layers indicate changes to the environment which have occurred over time. Sedimentary rocks can contain fossils because, unlike most igneous and metamorphic rocks, they form at temperatures and pressures that do not destroy fossil remnants.

1.2.3 *Metamorphic Rocks*

Metamorphic rocks arise from the transformation of existing rock types, in a process called metamorphism, which means "change in form". The original rock is subjected to heat (temperatures greater than 150 to 200°C) and pressure (1500 bars), causing profound physical and/or chemical change. The original rock may be a sedimentary rock, an igneous rock or another older metamorphic rock.

Metamorphic rocks make up a large part of the Earth's crust and are classified by texture and by chemical and mineral assemblage. They may be formed simply by being deep beneath the Earth's surface, subjected to high temperatures and the great pressure of the rock layers above it. They can form from tectonic processes such as continental collisions, which cause horizontal pressure, friction and distortion. They are also formed when rock is heated up by the intrusion of hot molten rock called magma from the Earth's interior. The study of metamorphic rocks (now exposed at the Earth's surface following erosion and uplift) provides information about the temperatures and pressures that occur at great depths within the Earth's crust. Some examples of metamorphic rocks are gneiss, slate, marble, schist, and quartzite.

1.3 Deccan Volcanic Province (DVP) of India

Deccan Volcanic Province (DVP) of India is one of the world's 10 large igneous provinces (LIPs) and perhaps the best studied Continental Flood Basalt (CFB). However, its genesis and evolution are still poorly understood. The DVP is one of the Earth's giant continental flood basalts and has a total exposed area of about half a million square kilometers, between latitudes 16°–24° N and longitudes 70°–77° E (Figure 1.2). In the northwestern, central and southern Indian peninsula, the approximate volume of the DVP is about 2 × 10^6 km^3 and its estimated age is 64–65 Ma. It is generally believed that the DVP originated during Gondwanaland breakup as part of the Seychelles-India separation event. Another important belief concerning this CFB is that it is the "head" of a plume which is currently active as Reunion volcanism, with the "tail" consisting of the rather irregular chain of volcanic islands extending from Reunion to and along the Laccadive-Maldive-Chagos ridges. The latter model has been refuted convincingly, as mentioned above. However, a viable alternative model has not yet been proposed.

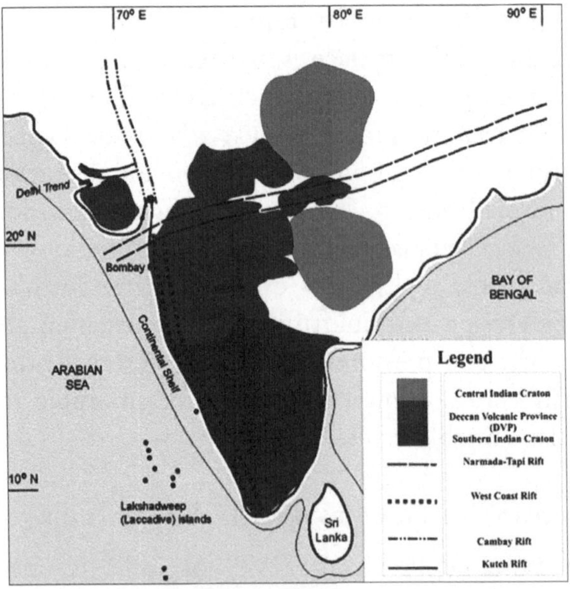

Fig. 1.2: Geological Map showing the Location of the Deccan Volcanic Province and its Relationship with the Geo-Tectonic Features of the Region (Modified after Sheth, 2005)

The DVP erupted on the Archean-Proterozoic shield areas of south, north-west and central India and the adjoining offshore area off the west coast (Devey and Stephens, 1991). The volcanics cover two cratonic areas—the Dharwar Craton of the south Indian shield and the central Indian craton. Apart from this, the DVP is associated with four major rift zones of peninsular India. It is juxtaposed with the east-west-running Narmada-Satpura-Tapti rift which is a horst-and-graben-type rift zone that trends ENE-WSW for > 1600 km along central India (Mishra, 1977). In northwest India, the DVP is in contact with the Cambay, Kutch and West Coast rifts

Recently, Sheth (2005) convincingly refuted the plume model as a basis for the genesis of the DVP. However, his suggestion that the DVP and Laccadive-Chagos ridge formed as a consequence of southward crack propagation along the Vishnu fracture zone is not consistent with data concerning the geo-magmatic and tectonic history of the Indian peninsular plate. The current status of knowledge thus represents a shortfall of understanding. The need to fill this gap in our knowledge, and to establish a genetic model for the DVP based on the vast volumes of existing scientific data, was the impetus for the present contribution.

The geochemical variation within the Deccan Volcanics, as mentioned above, perhaps indicates differences in the chemistry of the host rocks. For example, along the Narmada-Tapi rift zone the magmatic melt must have interacted with the host sediments, which are Mahakoshal Jurassics along with Archean metamorphics. Similarly along the West Coast, Cambay and Kutch rifts, the melt would have interacted with Archean-Precambrian metamorphics. Consequential changes in the chemistry would be reflected in the geochemistry of the DVP Volcanics.

Earth scientists from India and abroad carried out geological, geophysical, geochemical and dating, etc. to investigate the nature of Deccan Traps. Various thermo-physical properties, magnetic and electrical properties, etc. were measured at various temperature and physical conditions and published in various scientific journals (Gupta *et al.*, 1999). This has motivated me to compile the data on thermo-physical; magnetic, electrical and seismic properties, etc. of rocks in general and also specifically Deccan Traps generated by Indian scientists and update the information. The relationship among the various properties of rocks would motivate the earth scientists to do more work in this direction to interpret the field data using laboratory measurement data for the exploration of earth structure, nature of the earth, tectonics and natural mineral resources like oil, water, minerals and geothermal energy resources.

CHAPTER II

Thermal Properties of Rocks

The interior heat of the earth is transmitted to its surface mainly by three mechanisms: radiation, advection, and conduction. In the earth's lithosphere conduction of heat generally dominates among these mechanisms. The most important thermal properties of rocks are heat capacities, thermal conductivities sand thermal diffusivities. Data of measured thermal properties from rocks are used for assessment and evaluation of the heat flow from subsurface environments, Research in thermal properties of rocks is used for solving a number of other important problems including determination of natural thermal fields, research, exploration, development and exploitation of fossil fuels fields.

2.1 Definitions

2.1.1 *Thermal Conductivity*

Thermal Conductivity '*k*' is the property of a material that indicates its ability to conduct heat. It appears primarily in Fourier's Law of heat conduction.

2.1.2 *Fourier's Law of Conduction*

Fourier's law is an empirical law based on observation. It states that the rate of heat flow, dQ/dt, through a homogeneous solid is directly proportional to the area, A, of the section at right angles to the direction of heat flow, and to the temperature difference along the path of heat flow, dT/dx, i.e.

$$dQ/dt \propto A\, dT/dx \quad \ldots (2.1)$$

$$dQ/dt = k\, A\, dT/dx \quad \ldots (2.2)$$

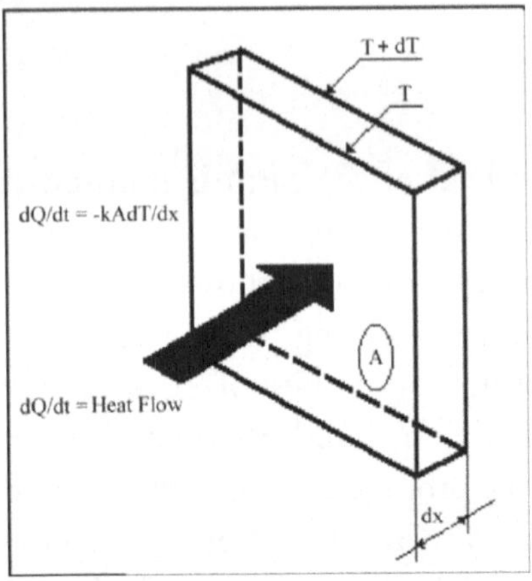

The proportionality constant, k, is called thermal conductivity of the material.

$$k = dQ/dt.\ A.\ dT/dx$$

Let $A = 1$, $dt = 1$, $dx = 1$ and $dT = 1$

So, Thermal conductivity is defined as the amount of heat per unit of time per unit area that is conducted through a slab of unit thickness of a material if the difference in temperature between opposite faces is one degree of temperature.

2.1.3 *Units*

Amount of heat is in Calories, '*A*' and '*x*' in CGS unit, '*T*' is in °C, and time in sec. Then the unit of thermal conductivity is Cal/cm'sec/°C and if it is in joules and temperature in Kelvin, '*A*' and '*x*' in MKS unit, then the unit is Watt/m/K.

2.2 Surface Heat Flow and Thermal Conductivity

Earth's evolution reflects the history of heat transfer from the interior via the fundamental processes of plate tectonics, conduction through continental lithosphere and hotspot volcanism. As a result, considerable attention has been directed toward the understanding Earth's thermal history, the variation in the temperature field in space and time. The primary directly observable quantity for surface heat flow is the temperature gradient near the surface, which is in turn used to estimate the flow of heat from the interior and hence draw inferences about the thermal structure and evolution.

Near the earth's surface, the temperature gradient is essentially vertical, so the outward heat flow Qs is the product of the vertical gradient of the temperature dTz/dz, which is most everywhere positive downwards (temperature increases with depth z), and the measured or estimated thermal conductivity of the material, k.

Surface heat flow (Qs) as defined the heat flow due to conduction from the earth surface per unit area per second can be expressed as,

$$Qs = -k\,(dTz/dz) \qquad \ldots (2.3)$$

Where, 'k' is the thermal conductivity. The negative sign indicates that the flow of heat from high to low temperature is upward.

In solids, thermal conduction is affected by free electrons and vibration of atoms. Thermal conductivity of rocks is greater than that of gases but about 100 times lesser than that of metals. Therefore most of the rocks and rock forming minerals are semiconductor of heat.

In semiconductors, the heat conduction is believed to be due to the linear molecular vibrations (Lattice Vibrations). At higher temperatures the lattice vibrations is higher while at lower temperatures the lattice vibrations diminishes. Bridgeman (1949) observed that the thermal conductivity of rocks increases with pressure at a rate of few percent per ten kbar. Kwada (1964, 1966) concluded that coefficient of thermal conductivity for most of the rocks and mineral decreases with temperature. At higher temperatures, radiative conduction also plays an important role. The expression can be written as (Carlslaw and Jeager, 1959):

$$k = k_l + k_r \qquad \text{... (2.4)}$$

$$= bf(p)/T + 16/3\,(n^2 K_B T^3)/\varepsilon_1 \qquad \text{... (2.5)}$$

Where

k = Effective thermal conductivity

$k_1 = b\,f(p)/T$ = Lattice conductivity (Lattice vibration)

$k_r = 16n^2 K_B\, T^3/3\varepsilon_1$ = Radiative conductivity

$b/T = k_0$ = Thermal conductivity under the normal perature conditions at earth's surface

$f(p)$ = 1 at the earth surface and 23 at the boundary between mantle and core (This expression depends upon pressure)

T = Temperature in Degree Kelvin

n = Effective index of refraction

K_B = Boltmann's constant

ε_1 = Opacity = $\varepsilon_0 + \varepsilon$ ... (2.6)

ε_0 = Opacity at low temperature

ε = Mean opacity.

At normal temperature—pressure conditions, thermal conduction in rocks depend upon porosity, density, mineral composition, grain size, etc. The lowest thermal conductivities are observed for loose materials i.e., dry sand, dry clay. Quartzite and rock salt have the highest conductivities. The same type of rock shows a broad range of conductivities. Electrons also play the dominant role in the conduction of heat. Since the motion of the electrons is much faster than that of atoms. Therefore, the thermal conductivity of non-metallic solids is usually much lower than that of metals.

Rocks generally have the coefficient of thermal conductivity ranges from 1 to 6 W m^{-1} K^{-1}. However, even within the same rock type, thermal conductivity can vary over a considerable range. Thermal conductivity at NTP of various types of rocks, water, ice, sand are shown in Figure 2.1.

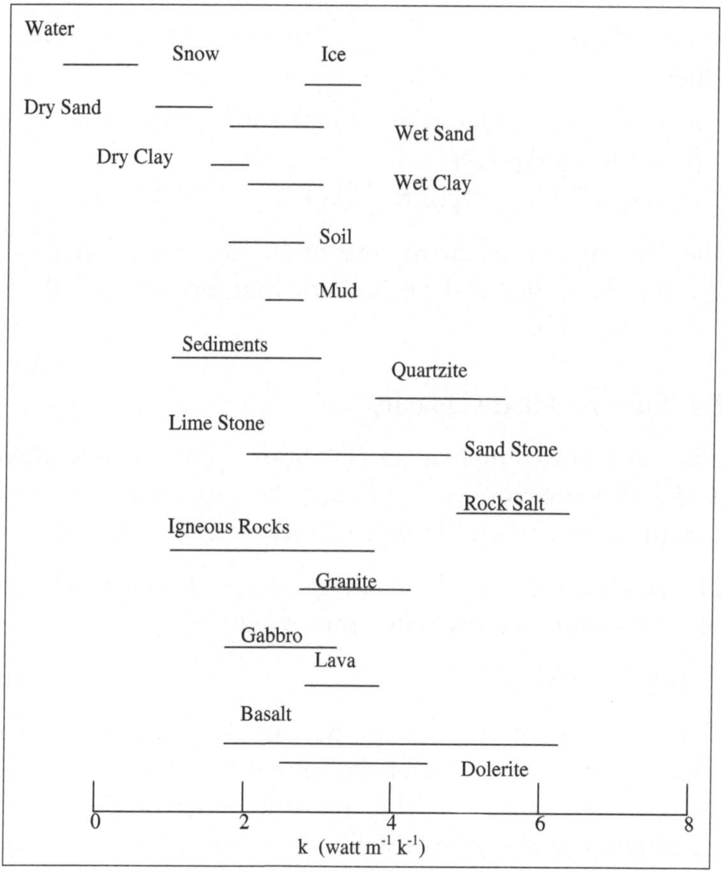

Fig. 2.1: Thermal Conductivities of Various Kinds of Rocks

2.3 Thermal Diffusivity

Thermal diffusivity (α) is a measure of the rate at which a temperature disturbance at one point in a body travels to another point. It is expressed by the relationship $k/\rho\ C_p$, where 'k' is the coefficient of thermal conductivity, ρ is the density, and C_p is the specific heat at constant pressure.

In heat transfer analysis, thermal diffusivity, α, is the ratio of thermal conductivity to volumetric heat capacity. It has the SI unit of m^2/s.

$$\alpha = k/\ C_p \qquad \ldots (2.7)$$

Where

k is thermal conductivity (SI units: W/(m·K))
ρ is density (kg/m^3)
C_p is specific heat capacity (J/(kgK))

The denominator of the thermal diffusivity expression above, C_p can be identified as the volumetric heat capacity with the SI unit of $J/(m^3{\cdot}K)$.

2.4 Specific Heat Capacity

It is also known simply as specific heat, *Cp,* is the measure of the heat energy required to increase the temperature of a unit quantity of a substance by a certain temperature interval.

The equation relating heat energy to specific heat capacity, where the unit quantity is in terms of mass is:

$$\Delta Q = mCp\Delta T \qquad \ldots (2.8)$$

Where ΔQ is the heat energy put into or taken out of the substance, m is the mass of the substance, Cp is the specific heat capacity, and ΔT is the temperature differential where the initial temperature of the reaction is subtracted from the final temperature. Heat capacity is usually expressed in units of cal/g°C in C.G.S system and $Jkg^{-1}K^{-1}$ in M.K.S system.

In the measurement of physical properties, the term specific denotes a bulk property an intensive property in which the value is independent of the quantity of substance. Specific heat capacity is unlike the "total" heat capacity (also called thermal mass) of a body an extensive property which is affected by the quantity of substance, and increases with the amount of the substance. More heat energy is required to increase the temperature of a substance with high specific heat capacity than one with low specific heat capacity. The specific heat capacities of many substances under many conditions have been quantitatively predicted by the quantum theory of interactions between particles which constitute the substances.

2.5 Measurement Techniques

Thermal parameters can be measured practically using either steady state or transient fields. The thermal parameters of interest are (1) Thermal conductivity 'k' (2) Thermal diffusivity 'α', and (3) the specific heat 'C_p'. All the three parameters are interrelated by the relation $\alpha = k/\rho\ C_p$ where 'ρ' is the density of rocks. Knowledge of any two determines the third.

2.5.1 *Measurements of Thermal Conductivity of Rocks*

Laboratory measurements of thermal conductivity of rocks can be divided into two parts (1) Direct measurements techniques using either steady state or transient temperature fields and (2) indirect measurement techniques using the relationship $\alpha = k/\rho\ C_p$ by measuring α, ρ and C_p.

Measurement Techniques: Measurement techniques of theses thermal properties are well described in literature. However, the measurement techniques commonly used for the measurement of thermal conductivity is described in brief.

2.5.1.1 *Direct Measurement Techniques*

These techniques may be further classified as follows:

1. Divided Bar Technique,
2. The Needle Probe Technique, and
3. Cut core method.

2.5.1.2 *Divided Bar Technique*

It is the most commonly used technique using steady state temperature field for the measurement of thermal conductivity of all types of rocks. Initially the apparatus is described by Benfield (1939). It has been modified by Beck (1957), Gupta and Rao (1970) so as to improve precise measurement and performance.

In this method, a sample material and a standard material, both in the form of plates are brought face to face in close contact and a steady heat flow is sent through them. From the measured values of temperature gradients in the two plates and from the known thermal conductivity of the standard material thermal conductivity of the sample material can be obtained by using the formula:

$$k_r = k_s (\Delta T_s / d_s)\ (dr / \Delta T_r) \qquad \ldots (2.9)$$

Where 'k_s' is the thermal conductivity of standard material, ΔT_s and ΔT_r the temperature differences between two plates between the two faces and *ds* and *dr* are the thicknesses of standard and unknown substances.

2.5.1.3 *Needle Probe Method*

In contrast with the steady state methods, transient methods are fast. The method is most commonly used, is the Transient line heat source (Needle Probe). This was given by Von Herzen (1959), Gupta (1960), Cull (1974), Bouguerra *et al.* (1997),

Manohar *et al.* (2000). In this method, a line heat source and a temperature sensitive device is used. Constant power is supplied to the heater and rise in temperature is recorded during the short heating interval. The thermal conductivity can be calculated from temperature-time record and the power input by using the following formula,

$$k = (Q/4\Delta T) \log (t_2/t_1) \qquad \dots (2.10)$$

Where Q is the power input by which ΔT is the temperature rise between time t_1 and t_2. Graph is plotted between ΔT and $\log (t_2/t_1)$, the slope of the plotted straight line will be $Q/4\pi k$.

Hence,

$$\text{Tan}\ \theta = Q/4\pi k$$

This technique is most suitable for soft materials i.e. sedimentary rocks and unconsolidated material.

2.5.1.4 *Cut Core Method*

Mongelli (1969) proposed this method for the measurement of thermal conductivity of rocks. In this method, the cylindrical sample is cut into equal parts and between these parts a flat heater in the spiral form is placed. Through this heater, current is sent and at a distance of 1–2 cm from cut, a thermo element is placed inside the core to measure temperatures. This method can be used for all types of rocks other than consolidated material.

2.5.1.5 *Thermal Conductivity of Mineral and Rocks*

Thermal properties of rocks and minerals are summarized and tabulated at time to time in several hand books and research publications (Clark, 1966, Horai, 1971, Kappelmeyer and Haenel, 1974, Cermak and Rybach, 1982, Gupta *et al.*, 1987, Gupta *et al.*, 1991, Brigand *et al.*, 1992, Gupta *et al.*, 1993,

Schon, 1996, Roy and Rao, 2000, Ray *et al.*, 2007). We have taken selected values of thermal conductivity of mineral and rocks from the various hand books and updated the values taking from the latest publications. Most of data has been compiled from Cermak and Rybach, 1982, Gupta *et al.*, 1987, 91 and 93, Roy and Rao 2000, and other publications referred in the table. The basalts from the Deccan Traps hot spring and other locations have also been shown in Table 2.1.

Thermal conductivity depends on many properties of a material, notably its structure and temperature. For instance, pure crystalline substances exhibit very different thermal conductivities along different crystal axes, due to differences in phonon coupling along a given crystal axis. Sapphire is a notable example of variable thermal conductivity based on orientation and temperature, with 35 W/(mK) along the c-axis and 32 W/(mK) along the a-axis.

2.5.2 *The Measurement of Thermal Diffusivity of Rocks*

Knowledge of the thermal diffusivity of a rock body is required for the prediction of its response to a transient heat source. Thermal diffusivity of a rock can be obtained indirectly from measurement of its conductivity, density and specific heat; indirectly by modelling, using assumed values of those parameters for each of its mineral constituents; indirectly by measurement of one or two parameters and assuming values for the remainder; or by direct measurement. The relatively unknown factor in the indirect methods is specific heat, which cannot be assumed to be constant, particularly in minerals that are members of a range of chemical mixtures.

Specific heat measured for a rock is generally higher than that modeled from the individual specific heats of the mineral components of the rock. Hence, direct measurement is

Table 2.1: Values of Thermal Conductivity of Rocks and Minerals from Various References

Mineral/Rocks	*N*	*K, Range* $Wm^{-1}\ k^{-1}$	*Mean,* $Wm^{-1}\ k^{-1}$	*Reference*
Carbonates	–	3.57	–	Cermak and Rybach, 1982
Quartz (001)	–	13.93	–	Kanamori *et al.*, 1968
Granite (Pink) Hyderabad, India Granite (grey) Tusham, India	20 10	3.16–3.66 3.08–3.99	3.42	Gupta *et al.*, 1987 Sundar *et al.*, 1990
Quartzite, Tusham, India	7	3.62–4.55	4.14	Sundar *et al.*, 1990
Granite-Gneiss, Eastern Dharwar, India	46	2.8–0–3.7	3.2	Gupta *et al.*, 1991
Granite, Bastar craton, India	5	3.35–4.08	3.69	Gupta *et al.*, 1993
Granite, Korea	10	1.96– 3.86	2.81	Kim *et al.*, 2007
Granite, Germany	11	2.5–4.03	3.10	Schon, 1996
Kola Peninsula,USSR	22	2.4–3.33	2.88	Schon, 1996
New South Wales, Australia	48	2.7–4.5	3.57	Beck, 1965
Granodiorite, NE USA	5	2.6–2.9	2.78	Birch,1966
Granodiorite, West Australia	9	1.6–2.3	2.03	Cermak and Rybach 1982
Diorite, USSR	46	1.8–2.8	2.26	Schon, 1996
Gabro, Baltic Shield, USSR	38	2.3–2.9	2.61	Schon, 1996
Anorthosite, Tranivaal, South Africa	25	1.6–1.9	1.76	Birch,1966

(Table contd…)

(Table 2.1 contd…)

Mineral/Rocks	*N*	*K, Range* $Wm^{-1} k^{-1}$	*Mean,* $Wm^{-1} k^{-1}$	*Reference*
Peridotite, USSR	14	3.8–4.9	4.37	Schon, 1996
Deccan Basalts:				
Koyna (Earthquake zone)	22	1.51–1.94	1.723182	Sharma, 1982
Latur (Earthquake zone)	82	1.67– 1.70	1.68	Roy and Rao, 2000
Ganeshpuri (Hot springs zone)	4	1.50–1.74	1.6325	Sharma, 1982
Unhavare (Hot springs zone)	5	1.84– 2.05	1.964	Sharma, 1982
Ahmadnagar area	130	1.59–1.85		Roy and Rao, 2000
Pune Area	116	1.68–1.82		Roy and Rao, 2000
Wardha area	28	1.61–1.68	1.64	Roy and Rao, 2000
Yavatmal Area	38	1.58–1.70		Roy and Rao, 2000

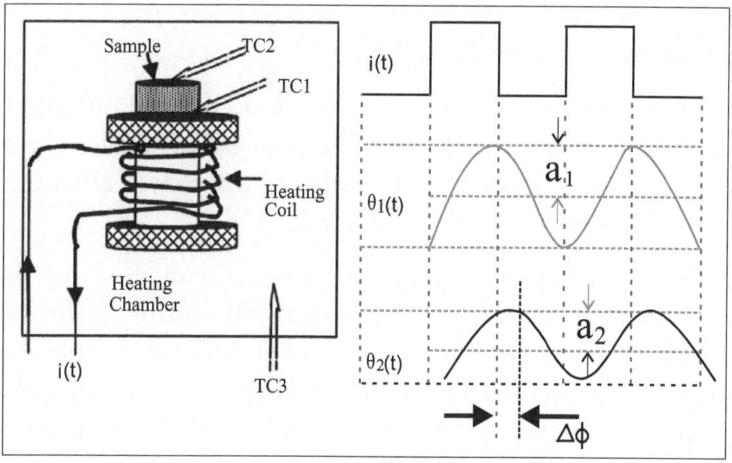

Fig. 2.2: Schematic illustration of the modified Angstrom method for measurements of thermal diffusivity. Amplitude ratio a_2/a_1 and phase shift $\Delta\phi$ of temperature θ_0 and θ_1 at both ends of the sample are measured to determine diffusivity. T is the period of heating current (After Kanamori *et al.*, 1968).

preferred. It is desirable to measure conductivity and diffusivity of the same sample. Kanamori *et al.* (1968) measured thermal diffusivity of rock forming minerals from 300 to 1100 K by modifying the Angstrom method (Carlslaw and Jaeger, 1959). The modified Angstrom method is shown schematically (Kanamori *et al.*, 1968) in Figure 2.2. This modified method allows diffusivity to be measured of rock disks that have been cut to meet the requirements of the divided bar apparatus for conductivity determinations. A thin sample disk is attached to a long matching rod of similar material, and diffusivity is obtained by measuring the amplitude decrement and phase lag of a sinusoidal temperature wave that travels through the assembly. The following equations derived by solving the basic equation of heat conduction in a cylindrical sample to calculate the thermal diffusivity '$\propto$',

$$\propto = \pi/\alpha_1\beta_1 T \qquad \dots (2.11)$$

where, the ratio of amplitude, $a_2/a_1 = 2\exp(-\alpha_1 l)$
and phase difference $\Delta\Phi = \beta_1 l$

A correction is made for the effect of thermal mismatch between disk and rod. Tests using standard materials suggest that diffusivity can be measured with an accuracy of ± 5%, and a repeatability of 3% (Kanamori *et al.*, 1968).

As mentioned above, Angstroms devised a method for the measurement of thermal diffusivity of small dimension samples. This method had been used globally to measure this property on rocks/minerals/carbon fibers/composites, etc. by modifying the system as per the requirements. Conventional experimental setup employs chart recorders to record the temperature traces as a function of time. The accuracy in calculation of thermal diffusivity depends on the accuracy and sensitivity of recorders. As the data is not collected in digital form, it was not possible to employ computers with suitable software to determine amplitudes of thermal waves and phase difference from experimental data in an error free automatic manner. Gopal and Sharma (2011) also modified the Angstrom method (Carlslaw and Jaeger, 1959) and developed software for the measurement of thermal diffusivity of rocks and minerals. A technique (process) is designed and developed where microprocessor based signal conditioners are used for the measurements of temperatures with advantage of signal stacking and linearization with the help of stored look up tables. Further more, window based software has been developed which has several features such as configuring signal conditioners, on screen monitoring of data being acquired in graphical as well as numerical form, smoothing of wave forms, automatic computation of waveform amplitudes and phase difference even when the wave forms are not ideal sine waves, using this improved thermal diffusivity apparatus (Figure 2.3). Thermal diffusivity of fused silica, corundum has been determined which are compatible with the reported values as shown in Table 2.2. Thermal diffusivity of some of the rocks from East Antarctica has also been determined by this method and are shown in Table 2.3.

Table 2.2: Results of Thermal Diffusivity Measurements on Some of the Standard Minerals and Comparison with the Reported Values

Mineral	*Thermal Diffusivity, 10^{-3} cm^2/s*		*Error*	*Reference*
	Measured	*Reported*		
Fused Silica (SiO_2)	7.28	7.23	0.4%	Kanamori *et al.*, 1968
Corundum (Al_2O_3)	64.2	66.0	2.7%	Cermak and Rybach, 1982

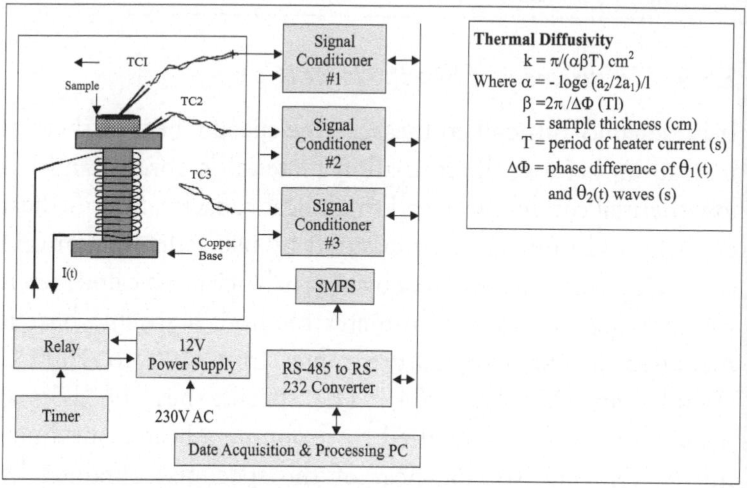

Fig. 2.3: Data processing window showing the original waveforms (raw data). This helps in quickly checking the data quality before performing other steps to compute thermal diffusivity. *TC*1, *TC*2, *TC*3 are thermal couples (Gopal and Sharma 2011).

Table 2.3: Thermal Diffusivity of the East Antarctica Samples

East Antarctica	
Rock Formation, Area	$\propto$, 10^{-7} m^2/s
Lenco gneiss, Scrimacher Oasis	7.69
Lenco gneiss Scrimacher Oasis	0.299
Gabro, N. humbolt	0.369
Lenco gneiss Scrimacher Oasis	8.25
Lenco geniss Scrimacher Oasis	8.88
Fined grained tonalite, S. humbolt	6.44
Lenco geniss, Scrimacher Oasis	6.18
Augen gneiss, Scrimacher Oasis	8.9
Charno kite, Scrimacher Oasis	6.35
Gneiss, Scrimacher Oasis	0.404

2.5.3 *Measurement of Specific Heat (Cp)*

It is generally difficult to measure the specific heat of thermal insulation, because the insulation material is porous, and has low thermal conductivity and small heat capacity. Specific heat of rocks and minerals are measured by using the relationship $\propto = k/\rho C_p$. It is also estimated by heat balance using calorimeter. By applying the drop calorimeter method, a specific heat is measured in the temperature range from 100 to 1000°C (Waples and Waples 2004). The specific heat of thermal insulation is simply measured by dropping a heated specimen into water. The specific heat of the specimen obtained by the apparatus is the "mean" specific heat between the initial specimen temperature before dropping and the equilibrium water temperature after dropping.

2.6 Temperature Effect on Thermal Properties of Rocks and Rock Forming Minerals

2.6.1 *Influence of Temperature on Thermal Conductivity*

Thermal conductivity is a function of temperature. Lattice (or phonon) thermal conductivity varies inversely with temperature. As thermal expansions increases with temperature, but differently for all minerals, "thermal cracking" by differential expansion may create contact resistances between mineral grains, thus contributing to the observed decrease of conductivity with temperature. This effect is probably not as severe in water-saturated rocks as it is in dry rocks, the condition in which most laboratory experiments are conducted. Conductivity-temperature determinations of crystalline water-saturated rocks are now under way in some laboratories.

The data on thermal conductivity as function of temperature on mineral and rocks was compiled by Clauser, and Huenges (1995 and references there in). It was observed that the thermal conductivity as a function of temperature is different in different rocks. However, it decreases with temperature initially, until around 1000–1200°C the radiative component balances and sometimes even inverts this decreasing trend.

Clauser and Huenges (1995) pointed out that for moderate temperatures k varies inversely with temperature. Based on the analysis of available data of thermal conductivity as function of temperature Zoth and Hanel (1988) suggest a relationship of the form,

$$k(T) = A + B/(350 + T) \qquad \ldots (2.12)$$

Where k is given in $Wm^{-1}K^{-1}$, T in °C, and the constants A and B are determined from a least square fit to measured data for different rock types as given by Clauser and Huenges (1995).

The effect of temperature on thermal conductivity of rocks has also been estimated using the relationship,

$$k(T) = k_o (1 + CT)^{-1} \quad \text{... (2.13)}$$

Where $k(T)$ and k_0 are the thermal conductivities at temperature $T(K)$ and at reference temperature. C is constant, which varies from $0.0006K^{-1}$ to $0.0014\ K^{-1}$ (Cermak and Rybach, 1982).

Table 2.4 shows the measurement on thermal diffusivity in the temperature range from 300 to 1100°K by Kanamori *et al.* (1968) on rock forming minerals other reported data on thermal properties on the same minerals. For all the minerals except feldspar thermal diffusivity decreases almost linearly with temperature up to 700°K, as expected from the theory of lattice conduction. Tightly packed minerals, such as periclase, spinel, and corundum, have diffusivity 3 to 10 times as large as that of other minerals. At temperatures higher than 700°K, thermal diffusivity increases with temperature for some minerals.

2.7 Relationship between Thermal Conductivity and Mineral Contents

Clauser and Huenges (1995) reviewed the data on thermal conductivity of rocks and minerals and other thermal properties. They summarize the results of their review and concluded that the modes temperatures and pressure there is a great variation of thermal conductivity which decreases significantly for temperatures and pressure above 300°C and 20MPa, respectively. As thermal conductivity for any specific rock type varies according to its mineral content, porosity, pore fluid, and anisotropy, a table of thermal conductivity purely according to rock type. They summarize the results of their review in two ternary diagram Figure 2.4 (A) and (B). These relate different types of rocks with those factors that have the

Table 2.4: Thermal Conductivity k (W m^{-1} k^{-1}, lower, number) and Thermal Diffusivity $\propto$ (10^{-7} m^2 s^{-1}, upper number) of some of the Minerals at Different Temperatures

Mineral		*Temperature, °K*								
		300	*400*	*500*	*600*	*700*	*800*	*900*	*1000*	*1100*
Quartz (001)	$\propto$ (10^{-2}cm²/sec)	7.14	3.57	2.38	1.69	1.37	1.14	1.41	1.54	1.64
ρ = 2.65 g/cm²	k (10^{-3} cal/cm/sec/°C)	13.93	8.20	6.24	4.81	3.91	3.56	3.87	4.56	5.15
Quartz (010)	$\propto$	3.33	2.00	1.45	1.15	0.96	0.89	1.00	1.14	1.28
ρ = 2.65 g/cm²	k	6.49	4.60	3.83	3.29	2.90	2.79	2.75	3.39	4.03
Fused silica (Fa_{x2}, Fa_{1x})	$\propto$	0.725	0.715	0.705	0.700	0.715	0.741	0.800	0.885	–
ρ = 2.21 g/cm²	k	1.147	1.384	1.499	1.612	1.725	1.854	2.060	2.323	–
Olivine (001)	$\propto$	1.85	1.49	1.22	1.08	1.03	1.04	1.09	1.2	1.35
ρ = 3.45 g/cm²	k	5.07	4.73	4.23	3.89	3.86	3.98	4.23	4.77	5.44
Periclase, MgO (001)	$\propto$	–	12.5	8.70	6.67	5.56	4.65	4.00	3.57	3.23
ρ = 3.58 g/cm²	k	–	46.05	34.12	27.21	23.19	19.63	17.12	15.61	14.32
Jadeite	$\propto$	1.54	1.28	1.11	0.97	0.88	0.84	0.83	0.89	0.96
		–	–	–	–	–	–	–	–	–
Granet (mean of 2)	$\propto$	1.10	1.00	0.91	0.85	0.81	0.79	0.80	0.81	0.83
		–	–	–	–	–	–	–	–	–
Spinel	$\propto$			34.5	31.3	28.6	25.6	24.4	22.5	21.8
Corundum	$\propto$		60.6	45.5	34.5	28.6	25.0	21.3	18.5	16.4
Alkali feldspar	$\propto$	7.09	6.67	6.49	6.71	6.99	7.30	7.81	8.33	8.96

most pronounced effect on their thermal conductivity. The position of a rock's name in the compositional triangle indicates ion a qualitative way its thermal conductivity. Metamorphic and plutonic rocks are made up of quartz, feldspars and mafic minerals and the contents of minerals from these three groups basically determine a rock's thermal conductivity. In volcanic and sedimentary rocks the third mineral component is replaced by air or water, as the high variability of porosity in these rocks is a major factor controlling their thermal conductivity.

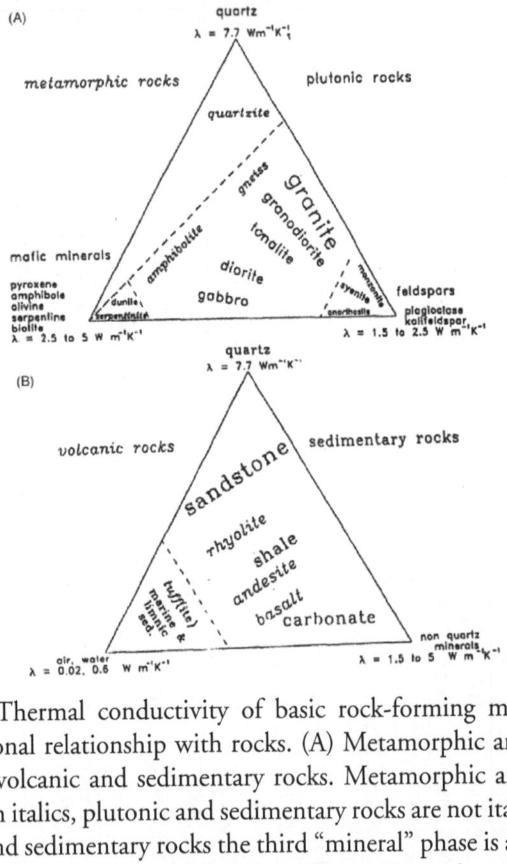

Fig. 2.4: Thermal conductivity of basic rock-forming minerals and compositional relationship with rocks. (A) Metamorphic and plutonic rocks (B) volcanic and sedimentary rocks. Metamorphic and volcanic rocks are in italics, plutonic and sedimentary rocks are not italicized. For volcanic and sedimentary rocks the third "mineral" phase is air or water, due to the great importance of porosity for the thermal conductivity of these rocks (After Clauser and Huenges, 1995).

2.7.1 *Thermal Conductivity and Porosity*

Surma and Geraud (2003) studied the relationship between porosity and thermal conductivity in case of granite. They observed that the relationship is not obvious and has to be studied in details. However they concluded that an increase of conductivity with a decrease of porosity, increase of conductivity related to an increase of fracture density).The study on different types of granite: altered, fractured or both indicated that parameters such as thermal conductivity are linked to the porous medium, the structure and the mineralogy of the rock.

2.8 Applications

2.8.1 *Temperature Inside the Earth*

Thermal properties are very important for the estimation of temperature inside the earth. This can be done using the Fourier's heat conduction equation,

$$dT/dt = k/\rho C_p \, d^2T/dz^2 \qquad \text{... (2.14)}$$

$$dT/dt = \propto d^2T/dz^2 \qquad \text{... (2.15)}$$

This is also called diffusion equation.

Three dimensional heat conduction equation can be written as,

$$\delta T/\delta t = \kappa(\delta^2 T/\delta x^2 + \delta^2 T/\delta y^2 + \delta^2 T/\delta z^2) \qquad \text{... (2.16)}$$

$$\delta T/\delta t = \kappa \, \nabla^2 T \qquad \text{... (2.17)}$$

The continental geothermal for a given region could be reasonably drawn if the parameters, namely surface heat flow, radiogenic heat source distribution, variation of thermal conductivity and mode of heat transfer within the lithosphere, are known. In a thermal sense, the lithosphere is commonly defined as an outer layer of the earth in which heat transfer is dominated by conduction, and the base of which is characterized by a temperature that a high enough to generate substantial amount of melt if the composition permits (Lachenbruch and Sass, 1978).

The one-dimensional steady state lithosphere temperature in a conductive regime in a homogeneous and isotropic medium, having 'A' as the heat production rate per unit volume, can be obtained by the solution of the Poisson's equation,

$$\nabla^2 T = d^2T/dZ^2 = -A/k \qquad \dots (2.18)$$

Where Z is the depth and k is the thermal conductivity of the medium.

The solution of eqn. (1) for the boundary conductions that Q_s is the heat flux at the surface and A_0, is the radioactive heat production in the top layers is given by (Gupta *et al.*, 1991):

$$T(z) = T_s + QZ/k - A_0Z^2/2k \qquad \dots (2.19)$$

Where T_s is the surface temperature.

In the case of a stratified structure, the temperature throughout and the heat flow (Q_i) at the bottom of the top layer of thickness Z_i, thermal conductivity k_i, and heat production A_i are given by (Sharma *et al.*, 2005).

$$T_i = T_s + (Q_i/k_i)Z_i - A_iZ_i^2/2k_i \qquad \dots (2.20)$$

$$Q_i = Q_{i-1} + A_iZ_i \qquad \dots (2.21)$$

Where i = 1, 2, 3–n and A_i is the radiogenic heat production in the ith layer.

The temperature effect on thermal conductivity can also be calculated using the relationship $k_T = k_0\,(1 + CT)^{-1}$ where k_T and k_0 are the values of thermal conductivity at temperature $T(K)$ and reference temperature and C is constant which varies from 0.0006 K^{-1} to 0.0014 K^{-1} (Cermak and Rybach, 1982).

Below the crust, if the mantle heat production is assumed to be negligible (Jones, 1988) the temperature at depth Z is given by (Gupta *et al.*, 1991),

$$T(z) = T(Z_m) + ((Z - Z_m)/k_m)/Q_m \quad \ldots (2.22)$$

Where Z_m and Q_m are the Moho depth and Moho heat flow respectively, and $T(Z_m)$ is the temperature at the Moho.

Birch *et al.* (1968) and Lachenbruch (1968) established the following linear relationship between surface heat flow (Q_s) and radioactive heat generation (A_0) in the surface rocks,

$$Q_s = Q_r + A_0 D \quad \ldots (2.23)$$

Where, Q_r is the reduced heat flow and 'D' is the characteristic depth—the thickness of the top radioactive layer. There are innumerable solutions for distribution of radioactive heat generation versus depth which can satisfy this emperical relationship (Gupta and Sharma, 1979). However the two extreme distributions that have been well discussed and preferred (Birch *et al.*, 1968, Roy *et al.*, 1968; Hyndman *et al.*, 1969; Lachenbruch, 1968) are: a constant heat generation to the depth 'D' (the step model) and the heat production decreasing exponentially with logarithmic decrement 'D' according to the relation,

$$A(Z) = A_0 e^{-Z/D} \quad \ldots (2.24)$$

Where 'Z' is the depth.

The subsurface temperatures, using exponential model where radioactive heat production in crust decreases with depth exponentially, can be estimated using the following expression (Lachenbruch, 1968, 1970).

$$T(z) = T_s + Q_s Z/K + A_0 D^2 (1 - e^{-Z/D})/k \quad \ldots (2.25)$$

2.8.2 *Earth Age*

Considering that the earth is slowing cooling by the process of heat conduction, the earth's age can be determined from the solution of the one dimension heat conduction equation (Carlslaw and Jaeger, 1959),

$$\rho c\,(\delta T/\delta t) = \delta/\delta z(k\delta T/\delta z) \qquad \dots (2.26)$$

In this equation ρ is the density, *c* is the specific heat and *k* the thermal conductivity of the cooling body. These parameters are known for particular rocks types, but Kelvin had to adopt generalized values for the entire Earth. The model assumes that the Earth initially had a uniform temperature T_0 throughout, and that it cooled from the outside leaving the present internal temperatures higher than the surface temperature. After a time '*t*' has elapsed the temperature gradient at the surface of the Earth calculated from the above equation is given by,

$$(dT/dz)_{z=0} = \sqrt{\rho c/\pi k}\; T_0/\sqrt{t} \qquad \dots (2.27)$$

Kelvin assumed an initial temperature of 7000 °F (3871 °C, 4144 K) for the hot Earth, and contemporary values for the surface temperature gradient and thermal parameters. The calculation for *t* yielded an age of about 100 Ma for the cooling Earth.

2.8.3 *Penetration of External Heat into the Earth*

The surface temperature of the earth varies cylindrically. Suppose it varies with angular frequency ω. The solution of the heat conduction equation with the boundary conditions of the surface for a surface temperature variation with depth '*Z*' in time '*t*' (Lowrie,1997) is

$$T(Z, t) = T_0 e^{-Z/d} \cos(\omega t - Z/d) \qquad \dots (2.28)$$

Where T_0 is the surface temperature and $d = (2\propto/\omega)^{1/2}$ is the decay depth of the temperature and '∝' is the thermal diffusivity of the earth' material. At this depth the amplitude of the temperature fluctuation is attenuated to $1/e$ of its value at surface temperature. At a depth of $5d$ the amplitude is less than 1% of the surface value and is effectively zero. d is inversely proportional to the frequency, so long period fluctuations penetrates more deeply than rapid fluctuations.

For crustal rocks, R = 2.65 kg $m^{-3;}$ thermal conductivity = 2.5 $Wm^{-1}K^{-1}$; and specific heat, C_p = 700 $Jkg^{-1}K^{-1}$. These give thermal diffusivity, $\propto = 1.25 \times 10^{-6}\ m^2\ s^{-1}$. The diurnal temperature variation (period 86, 400s) has $\omega = 7 \times 10^{-5} s^{-1}$. The daily temperature variation has negligible effect deeper than about a meter. Similarly, the annual temperature variation accompanying seasonal changes has a penetration depth of 3.8 m and is negligible deeper than 19 m. So heat flow measurements made within 20 m of the surface will be falsified by the daily and annual variations of surface temperatures.

Considering the diurnal variation, the shallow thermal surveys (Temperature measurement at a depth of 1 m or more) have been carried out for the exploration of geothermal resources in Pugga (Laddak) (Gupta *et al.*, 1983), west coast hot spring areas (Sharma and Gupta, 1978), Garampani (Asam) (Sharma *et al.*, 1982) and also in Mukunda fire zone, Jharia coal field (Bihar) for the detection and delineation of areas of under ground mine fires (Gupta *et al.*, 1986).

CHAPTER III

Density, Porosity and Permeability

3.1 Introduction

The density, porosity and permeability of the rocks are very important factors for the exploration of ground water, hydrocarbon and geothermal resources. This chapter deals these physical properties. Apart from the measurement techniques and the factors influencing these properties, the usefulness of these properties has also been described.

3.2 Density

Knowledge of the distribution of underground rock densities can assist in interpreting subsurface geologic structure and rock type. Density varies significantly among different rock types because of differences in mineralogy and porosity.

Density (ρ) is defined as the mass (M) of a substance per unit volume (V) i.e. $\rho = M/V$. The bulk density is the average density including voids density 'ρ_v', matrix density 'ρ_m'; and fluid density 'ρ_p'. Though density is defined as the mass of a substance per unit volume; however, in common usage, it is taken to be the weight in air of a unit volume of a sample at a specific temperature. Weight is the force that gravitation exerts on a body (and thus varies with location), whereas mass (a measure of the matter in a body) is a fundamental property and is constant regardless of location. In routine density measurements of rocks, the sample weights are considered to be equivalent to their masses, because the discrepancy between weight and mass would result in less error on the computed density than the experimental errors introduced in the measurement of volume. Thus, density is often determined using weight rather than mass. Density should properly be reported in kilograms per cubic meter (kg/m^3), but is still often given in grams per cubic centimeter (g/cm^3).

Another property closely related to density is specific gravity. It is defined, as noted above, as the ratio of the weight or mass in air of a unit volume of material at a stated temperature to the weight or mass in air of a unit volume of distilled water at the same temperature. Specific gravity is dimensionless (*i.e.*, has no units).

It has a relatively narrow range of variation (1–3.4). The bulk density depends on mineral composition, porosity, and contents of voids. In magmatic and metamorphic rocks, it is essentially a function of the mineral density and it increases from acid to basic rocks. In sedimentary rocks it is essentially a function of the porosity and of the saturation. The density of some of the magmatic and metamorphic rocks is shown in Figure 3.1 and for sedimentary rocks; the density range is shown in Figure 3.2.

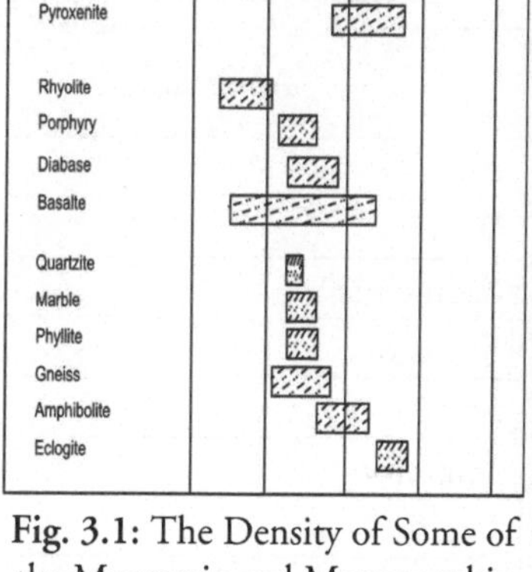

Fig. 3.1: The Density of Some of the Magmatic and Metamorphic Rocks (After Schon, 1996)

The relative variation in rock density is quite small,

and there is considerable overlap in the measured densities. Hence, knowledge of rock density alone will not be sufficient to determine rock type. The densities associated with various earth materials are shown in Table 3.1.

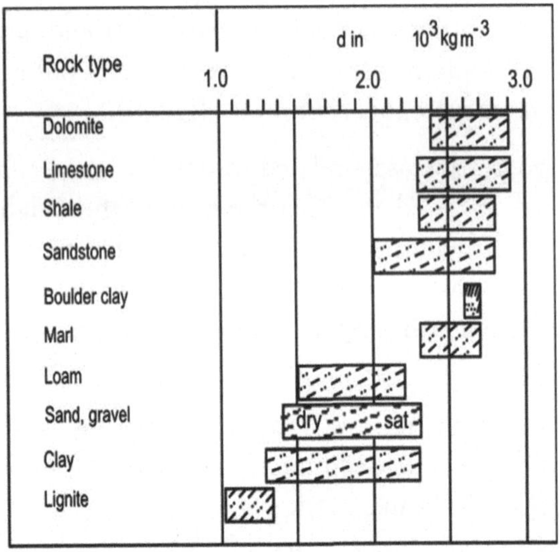

Fig. 3.2: Mean Density Range of Sedimentary Rocks (after Wohlenberg 1982)

Table 3.1: Densities Associated with Various Earth Materials

Material	*Density (gm/cm^3)*
Air	~0
Water	1
Sediments	1.7–2.3
Sandstone	2.0–2.6
Shale	2.0–2.7
Limestone	2.5–2.8
Granite	2.5–2.8
Basalts	2.7–3.1
Metamorphic Rocks	2.6–3.0

3.3 Porosity

The porosity of a rock, or sedimentary layer, is an important consideration when attempting to evaluate the potential volume of water or hydrocarbons it may contain. It is a measure of the void spaces in a material, and is a fraction of the volume of voids over the total volume, between 0–1, or as a percentage between 0–100%. Total porosity is defined as:

$$\Phi = 1 - Vm/V = Vp/V \quad \ldots (3.1)$$

Where, Vm is the volume of the matrix, V is the total volume of the material, and Vp is the volume of the pores This is dimensionless number and represented as percentage of the volume.

Porosity is a fraction between 0 and 1, typically ranging from less than 0.01 for solid granite to more than 0.5 for peat and clay. It may also be represented in percent terms by multiplying the fraction by 100.

Various kinds of porosity are defined as primary, secondary, inter-granular, inter-crystalline, fissures, etc. and discussed below.

3.4 Types of Porosities

3.4.1 *Primary Porosity*

It is the main or original porosity system in a rock or unconfined alluvial deposit.

3.4.2 *Secondary Porosity*

It is a subsequent or separate porosity system in a rock, often enhancing overall porosity of a rock. This can be a result of chemical leeching of minerals or the generation of a fracture system. This can replace the primary porosity or coexist with it.

3.4.3 *Fracture Porosity*

This is porosity associated with a fracture system or faulting. This can create secondary porosity in rocks that otherwise would not be reservoirs for hydrocarbons due to their primary porosity being destroyed.

3.4.4 *Vuggy Porosity*

This is secondary porosity generated by dissolution of large features (such as macrofossils) in carbonate rocks leaving large holes, vugs, or even caves.

3.4.5 *Effective Porosity*

It is also called open porosity and refers to the fraction of the total volume in which fluid flow is effectively taking place (this excludes dead-end pores or non-connected cavities). This is very important for groundwater and petroleum flow, as well as for solute transport.

3.4.6 *Dual Porosity*

It refers to the conceptual idea that there are two overlapping reservoirs which interact. In fractured rock aquifers, the rock mass and fractures are often simulated as being two overlapping but distinct bodies. Delayed yield, and leaky aquifer flow solutions are both mathematically similar solutions to that obtained for dual porosity; in all three cases water comes from two mathematically different reservoirs (whether or not they are physically different).

3.4.7 *Macro Porosity*

It refers to pores greater than 50 nm in diameter. Flow through macropores is described by bulk diffusion.

3.4.8 *Meso Porosity*

It refers to pores greater than 2 nm and less than 50 nm in diameter. Flow through mesopores is described by Knudsen diffusion.

3.4.9 *Micro Porosity*

It refers to pores smaller than 2 nm in diameter. Movement in micro pores is by activated diffusion.

Porosity is extremely variable and hardly systematic, but a general trend can be observed among earth materials as given below. Porosity generally decreases with increasing age and depth.

High Porosity	*Highly Porous Marine Sediments*
↑	Unconsolidated sediments (porosity decreases from clay to silt to sand to gravel)
	Sandstones
↓	Carbonate rocks
Low porosity	Fractured igneous rocks and other initially "dense" rocks type

3.5 Permeability

Permeability is a measure of the ability of a porous material to transmit the fluid, and is defined by Darcy's law as the proportionality constant relating the volume flow rate q for a incompressible fluid of viscosity 'μ' to the pressure gradient ∇P, driving the flow (Wang et al., 2004, Whitaker, 1986), as,

$$q = -kA.\ \nabla P/\mu \qquad \ldots (3.2)$$

$$k = q\ \mu/A\nabla P \qquad \ldots (3.3)$$

Where k is the permeability, A is the total cross sectional area of the porous material. Permeability is determined by measuring the fluid pressure difference across a sample and the resulting flow rate through it.

3.5.1 Units

Darcy (d), in S.I., it is m^2 (μm^2), $1d = 0.9869\ \mu m^2$

In most practical cases 1d = 19869 μm^2

Permeability depends on porosity, pore size and distribution, pore shape, arrangement of pores and pore throats. It can vary by 13 orders of magnitude. Value of '*k*' increases with increase in porosity and grain size and decreases with increase in degrees of compaction and cementation. The range of permeability in rocks is shown in Figure 3.3 (Nelson, 1985).

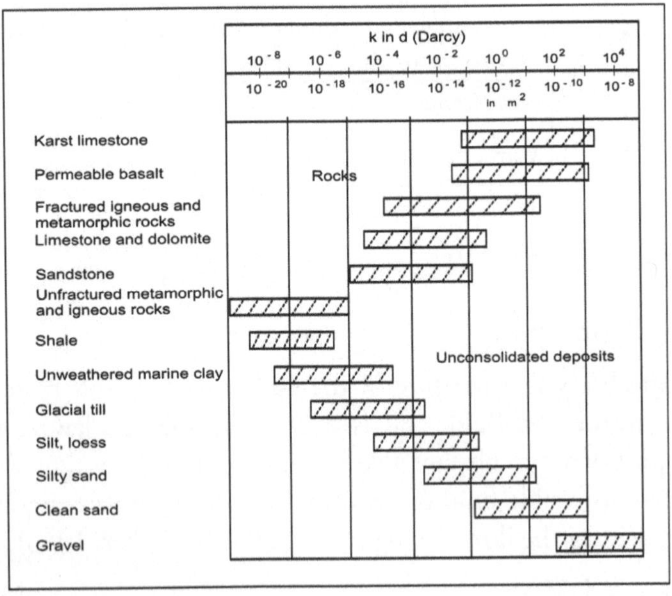

Fig. 3.3: Range of Permeability Values in Rocks (after Nelson 1985). Note that the Scale Spans 13 Orders of Magnitude.

3.6 Laboratory Measurements

3.6.1 Density

There are various methods like Vernier Callipers, non-wetting fluid displacement and Archimedes, etc., for the measurements of bulk volume for the determination of density of rocks. Among all the methods, Archimedes method is most commonly used for the estimation of density of the rocks.

In Archimedes method, the sample is weighed dry, fully saturated with formation brine whose density is accurately known. The saturated sample is then weighed suspended under a balance in air, and again while suspended in the fluid in which it is saturated. The various weight readings and the density of the fluid allow the bulk volume of any irregular sample to be found accurately. The difference in the weight between the saturated sample suspended in air and that when suspended in the fluid is equal to $Vs\rho_f$, where ρ_f is the density of the fluid. There are few sources of significant error in this method, provided no fluid drains from the plug whilst it is weighed in air.

For practical purpose, specific gravity is measured. Specific gravity is a dimensionless number (no units), and is the ratio of the weight of a rock to the weight of an equal volume of water. There is no difference between the two.

The formula is as follows:

$$\text{Density} = \frac{(\text{Weight in air})}{(\text{Weight in air}) - (\text{Weight in water})}$$

Water has a density of 1 g/cm^3, thus it buoys up anything within it by 1 gram per cubic centimeter of displacement. Because of this, the weight in air minus the weight in water, is equal to the volume of the rock sample.

Table 3.2: Density and Porosity of Deccan Basalts from Deccan Traps, Antarctica and Nagaland Regions

Area	*Rock formation*	*No. of Samples*	*Density Range kg/cm*	*Mean*	*Porosity Range %*	*Mean*
Latur (Deccan Trap)	Basalt, Flow 12	10	2.83–2.98	2.92 ± 0.05	0.03–1.97	0.661 ± 0.56
Latur (Deccan Trap)	Basalt, Flow 13	62	2.81–3.09	2.92 ± 0.05	0.03–2.55	0.812 ± 0.52
Nagaland	Basalt	25	2.78–3.33	2.99 ± 0.13	0.002–1.16	0.288 ± 0.30
Saurashtra (Deccan Trap)	Basalt	48	2.84–3.12	2.98 0.14	0.0114–3.9872	1.213 ± 1.09
East Antarctica		38	2.55–3.117	2.75 ± 0.12	0.002–1.16	0.208 ± 0.14
East Antarctica		10	2.55–2.79	2.68 ± 0.09	0.11–0.47	0.289 ± 0.10

Using Archimedes method, the density and porosity of the Deccan basalts from Latur Area (Maharastra) and Saurashtra region and other rock formations from Antarctica, Nagaland have been determined (Sharma *et al.*, 2004) and shown in Table 3.2.

3.6.2 *Porosity*

There are many methods for measuring porosity, a few of which will be discussed below.

3.6.2.1 *Imbibition Method*

The rock sample is immersed in a wetting fluid until it is fully saturated. The sample is weighed before and after the imbibition, and if the density of the fluid ρ is known, then the difference in weight is V_p, and the pore volume V_p can be calculated. The bulk volume V is measured using either Vernier Callipers and assuming that the sample is perfectly cylindrical, or by Archimedes Method (discussed later), or by fluid displacement using the saturated sample. V_p and V can then be used to calculate the connected porosity. This is an accurate method that leaves the sample fully saturated and ready for further petro–physical tests. The time required for saturation depends upon the rock permeability.

3.6.2.2 *Mercury Injection*

The rock is evacuated, and then immersed in mercury. At laboratory pressures mercury will not enter the pores of most rocks. The displacement of the mercury can therefore be used to calculate the bulk volume of the rock. The pressure on the mercury is then raised in a stepwise fashion, forcing the mercury into the pores of the rock. If the pressure is sufficiently high, the mercury will invade all the pores. A measurement of the amount of mercury lost into the rock provides the pore volume directly.

The porosity can then be calculated from the bulk volume and the pore volume. Clearly this method also measures the connected porosity. In practice there is always a small pore volume that is not accessed by the mercury even at the highest pressures. This is pore volume that is in the form of the minutest pores. So the mercury injection method will give a lower porosity than the two methods described above. This is a moderately accurate method that has the advantage that it can be done on small irregular samples of rock, and the disadvantage that the sample must be disposed of safely after the test.

The mercury method also has the advantage that the grain size and pore throat size distribution of the rock can be calculated from the mercury intrusion pressure and mercury intrusion volume data. This will be discussed at further length in the section on capillary pressure.

3.6.2.3 *Density Methods*

If the rock is mono-mineralic, and the density of the mineral it is composed of is known, then the pore volume and porosity can be calculated directly from the mineral density and the dry weight of the sample. This method gives the total porosity of the rock, but is of no practical use in petro-physics.

3.6.2.4 *Petro-graphic Methods*

This method is used to calculate the two dimensional porosity of a sample, either by point counting under an optical microscope or SEM, or image analysis of the images produced from these microscopes. Commonly a high contrast medium is injected into the pores to improve the contract between pores and solid grains. This method can provide the total porosity, but is wildly inaccurate in all rocks except those that have an extremely isotropic pore structure. However, it has the advantage that pore types and the micro-textural properties of the rock can be determined during the process.

3.6.2.5 *Bulk Volume Measurement Method*

Most of the methods reviewed above require the knowledge of the bulk volume of the rock sample. Three ways are commonly used. These are:

1. by using callipers,
2. using fluid displacement, and
3. using Archimedes' method.

(i) Vernier Callipers

If the rock is a perfect right cylinder with smooth surfaces, then caliper measurements of length and diameter can give quite an accurate bulk volume. In this case several measurements (approx.10) are made of the length and the diameter, and the arithmetic mean of each is used. Repeatability and accuracy then depend mainly upon surface texture of the sample. Repeat helium expansion determinations of porosity on samples with smooth surface textures where the calliper bulk volume is used should fall within ±0.3 porosity percent regardless of actual porosity. Inaccuracies can arise with samples with very high permeability. High permeability sandstone samples are frequently friable, have large grain and pore sizes, and do not produce smooth surfaced right cylinders when plugs are drilled and accurate bulk volume determination becomes difficult. Straightforward measurement with Vernier Callipers is not possible and Archimedes method or other liquid displacement methods have to be used.

(ii) Fluid Displacement

This method notes the displacement of fluid on a graduated scale when the rock sample is placed in a container containing the fluid. If the fluid automatically enters the pores errors will result. The method is commonly carried out with a non-wetting fluid such as mercury, or with other fluids with a sample that has already been saturated. Mercury displacement is carried out in a pyknometer fitted with a calibrated pump (Kobe method). The sample is immersed in mercury during this test and will give erroneous results where mercury enters samples with very large pores. There is also a tendency to give high bulk volumes if air is trapped where the sample touches the top of the chamber. The Kobe method is used as the first part of the mercury injection method.

(iii) Archimedes' Method

The sample is weighed dry, fully saturated with formation brine whose density is accurately known. The saturated sample is then weighed suspended under a balance in air, and again while suspended in the fluid in which it is saturated. The various weight readings and the density of the fluid allow the bulk volume of any irregular sample to be found accurately. The difference in the weight between the saturated sample suspended in air and that when suspended in the fluid is equal to $Vs\rho_f$, where ρ_f is the density of the fluid.

Porosity of Deccan Basalts and rock samples from, East Antarctica, Nagaland regions estimated using Archimedes' Method is shown in Table 3.2. It should be noted that these are all laboratory methods. Well logging utilises several other different techniques, which all have larger errors associated with them. These are based on acoustic, electromagnetic, NMR, and radioactive processes.

3.7 Relationship between Porosity and Density

3.7.1 *Basalts from Deccan Trap Region*

The density and porosity of the Deccan basalts from two different flows (12 and 13) of Latur area, Maharastra have been determined and plotted and shown in Figure 3.4 (Sharma *et al.*, 2004). The figure shows that there is inverse correlation between density and porosity in basalts. Higher density basalts have low porosity and vice versa.

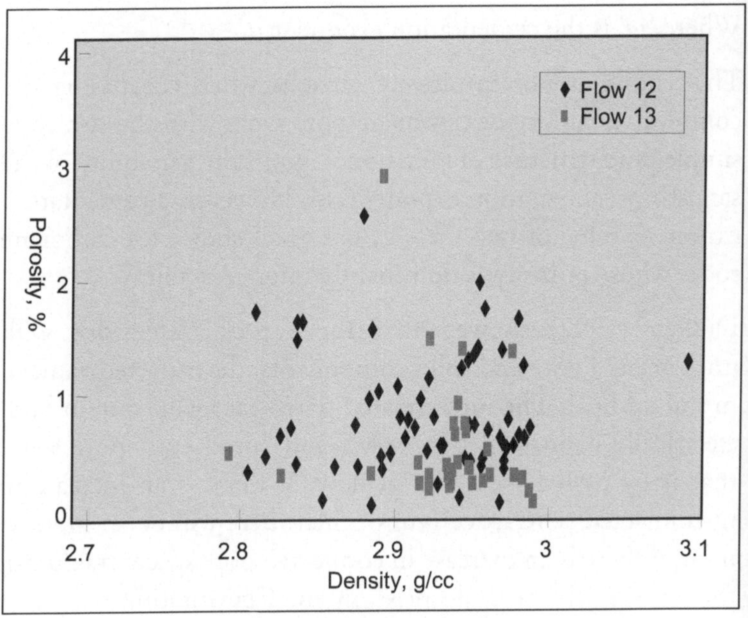

Fig. 3.4: Density-Porosity Relationships in Basalts from Latur Area, Maharastra

3.7.2 *Formation Factor—Porosity Relationships for Carbonates*

Porosity in sandstones generally takes the form of inter-granular pores: the pore space between the grains of quartz and other detrital minerals. In some cases there may be inter-crystalline porosity caused most commonly by calcite or quartz cement introduced by digenesis in the lithification of the sandstone. Porosity in carbonate rocks (limestones and dolomites) can take a wide variety of forms (Choquette and Pray, 1970).

The relationship between formation factor (F) and porosity (Φ) can be by Archie's equation. The most widely used form of the Archie's equation (1942) is,

$$F = 1/\Phi^{m} \quad \text{... (3.4)}$$

Where '*m*' is the cementation exponent

This choice is not intuitively obvious when comparing the complex variability of carbonate pore types with the relatively simple pore structure of sandstones, given the variability of the sandstone cementation exponent, m. However, a cementation exponent value of two ($m = 2$) is a good choice for carbonate rocks whose porosity is dominantly inter-crystalline.

Dullien (1992) showed that for a rock framework with uncorrelated pore and solid components, the expected value of m should be 2. The uncorrelated pore space will contain both electrically connected pore space and "dead end" pore space that is by-passed by electrical flow. If there is an increase in unconnected pore space (vugs), then there will be an increase in m; if there is an increase in connected pore space (fractures), then there will be a decrease in m. Cementation exponent 'm' varies from system to system. As a rule-of-thumb values of m quoted in the log analysis literature for various pore intergranular/intercrystalline 2.0, for fracture 1.4, for vugs 2.3 and for moldic, it is 3+.

Obviously, these numbers will be controlled by the degree of fracturing, vugginess and proportion of moldic porosity and can lead to a wide variety of m values observed in the field.

1
10

Formation factor, F
15

This relationship is shown in Figure 3.5.

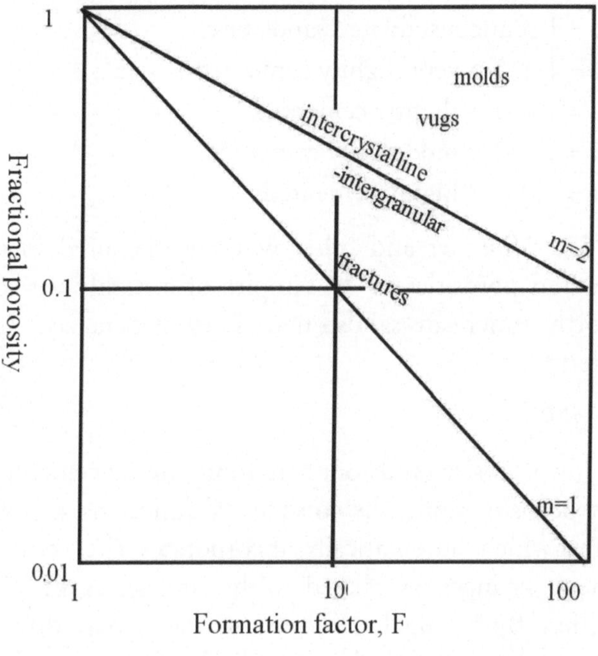

Fig. 3.5: Relationship between Formation Factor and Porosity for Carbonate Rocks (After Dullien, 1992)

3.7.3 *Formation Factor—Porosity Relationships for Sandstones*

Archie (1942) measured the formation factor of a variety of sandstones (a simple laboratory procedure involving a Wheatstone bridge) and compared these with their porosities to deduce the variation of m with type of sandstone. He found that m was 1.3 for unconsolidated sands and ranged between 1.8 and 2.0 for consolidated sandstones. Guyod gave the name cementation exponent to m, but noted that the pore geometry controls on m were complex and went beyond simple cementation. However, a useful rule-of-thumb comparative scale is widely quoted as:

- $m = 1.3$ unconsolidated sandstones
- $m = 1.4$–1.5 very slightly cemented
- $m = 1.6$–1.7 slightly cemented
- $m = 1.8$–1.9 moderately cemented
- $m = 2.0$–2.2 highly cemented

In 1952, Winsauer and other workers measured formation factors and porosities in 29 samples of a highly varied suite of North American sandstones. They generalized Archie's equation to:

$$F = a/\Phi^m \qquad \ldots (3.5)$$

Since low porosity sandstones are more highly cemented than higher porosity sands, the constant 'a' functions as a slippage element which automatically incorporates the cementation exponent changes associated with sandstones of differing porosities. By taking logarithms of both sides, this can be transformed to a straight line relationship:

$$\text{Log } F = \log a - m \log \Phi \qquad \ldots (3.6)$$

On fitting log F to log, they came up with a relationship for sandstones:

$$F = 0.62/\Phi^{2.15} \qquad \ldots (3.7)$$

Which is known as the "Humble equation" (since they worked for the Humble Oil Company) and is the most widely used equation for sandstones in the world.

3.8 Permeability and Hydrocarbons

Permeability is the most important single property of a hydrocarbon reservoir rock. Rock properties which influence permeability include particle size, particle packing, particle size distribution, grain angularity, and the degree of lithification (cementation and consolidation). Specific permeability of a porous media refers to a permeability measured with a single fluid at 100% saturation of that fluid present in the pore spaces. The effective permeability of a porous media applies to the permeability of each phase at a specified saturation when two or more phases are present in the pore spaces. Effective permeabilities are always lower than specific permeabilities because the presence of other phases inhibits the ability of a specific phase to flow.

3.9 Porosity and Permeability Relationship

Although there is no direct relationship between porosity and permeability, both of these rock properties are extremely important when assessing the reservoir potential of a given rock type. Porosity in volcanic rocks is mainly defined by the abundance of vesicles. In the case of pyroclastic rocks, grain size distribution and sorting determine the packing density of clasts. The porosity of a pyroclastic rock generally imparts a primary permeability; if subjected to hydrothermal fluid circulation, this permeability may change as a result of the dissolution of glass and the growth of secondary minerals. The porosity of pyroclastic rocks may reach 80%, but for fresh, non-altered pyroclastic rock, porosity is generally in the range of 40 to 60%. Lavas, on the other hand, exhibit porosity only if they are brecciated during emplacement or contain vesicles and other gas cavities such as lithophysae; in these cases, lava porosity is generally $< 20\%$.

The bulk permeability of volcanic rocks is a function of primary and secondary permeability. Primary permeability develops from the original texture of the rock. In contrast, secondary permeability (sometimes called *fracture permeability*) is promoted by rock fracture and foliation, and where it occurs; it is generally the dominant type of permeability. Volcanic rock fracture has numerous origins, such as tectonic movement and proximity to faults, differential compaction that causes stress fractures, cooling contractions, thermal spallation, and eruptive/emplacement brecciation. Typical permeabilities for all rock types range from 10^{-20} m^2 (0.01 μ Darcy) to 10^{-7} m^2.

Porosity and permeability are two of the primary factors that control the movement and storage of fluids in rocks and sediments. They are intrinsic characteristics of these geologic materials. The exploitation of natural resources, such as groundwater and petroleum, is partly dependent on the properties of porosity and permeability.

The range of values for permeability in geologic materials is extremely large. The most conductive materials have permeability values that are millions of times greater than the least permeable. Permeability is often directional in nature. The characteristics of the interstices of certain materials may cause the permeability to be significantly greater in one direction. Secondary porosity features, like fractures, frequently have significant impact on the permeability of the material. In addition to the characteristics of the host material, the viscosity and pressure of the fluid also affect the rate at which the fluid will flow.

3.10 Density, Porosity and other Thermo-Physical and Radioactive Properties

Thermo-physical and radioactive properties and their co-relations suggested by scientists based upon experimental data (Schon 1996).

3.10.1 *Density, Iron Content and Magnetic Susceptibility*

d = 33.7% (Fe content %) + 2583.5 kg/m^3

K = 0.0064 (Fe content) 1.71 (Swedish Malmborgit mines).

Imp.: No inverse co-relation between the susceptibility and the Fe_2O_3 content of rock exist

3.10.2 *Density and Radioactivity (Rybach and Cermak, 1982)*

For a rock series from trachites and granites to basalts and gabro

Ln A = 22.54 – 8.145.d and

A = d. (9.52.Cu + 2.56.CTh + 3.38 Ck%) μWm^{-3}

(C-Concentration in ppm for Uranium and Thorium and *Ck* is the *wt* content of Potassium (%), d is in kg/m^3).

3.10.3 *Density (d) and Compressional Wave Velocity (Vp) (Birch, 1961)*

V_p (km/s) = 2.76.d (g/cm^3) –0.98 (For magmatic rocks from North America)

V_p (km/s) = 2.67.d–1.08 (Magmatic rocks from USSR)

V_p (km/s) = 3.10.d ((g/cm^3) –0.98 (for plutonic rocks)

V_p (km/s) = 2.30.d ((g/cm^3) –0.91 (for volcanic rocks)

V_p (km/s) = 2.61.d ((g/cm^3) –0.1 ±0.4 (for mantle rocks)

3.10.4 *Density and Shear Wave Velocity (Gebrande et al., 1982)*

V_s (km/s) = 1.66.d ((g/cm^3)–1.48 (For plutonic rocks)

V_s (km/s) = 1.46.d ((g/cm^3)–1.02 (For volcanic rocks)

V_s (km/s) = 1.70.d ((g/cm^3)–1.62 (For metamorphic rocks)

3.10.5 *Compressional Wave Velocity and Porosity (Dortman, 1976)*

V_p (km/s) = 7.121 – 0.227ϕ (%) (for gabbro at 10 Mpa)

3.10.6 *Density and Thermal Conductivity (Horai, 1971)*

λ = 0.51–*d* 3.1 (d varies from 1.4 –3.0 g/cc)

3.10.7 *Density and Specific Heat (Schon 1996)*

Cp–*Cv* = (3 α*T*) 2β *T*/*d*

(α = Linear coefficient of thermal expansion, β = bulk modulus, *d* = density and *T* is temp in Kelvin)

CHAPTER IV Electrical Properties of Rocks

4.1 Introduction

There has been increasing interest in the electrical properties of rocks at depth within the Earth and the Moon. The reason for this interest has been consideration of the use of electrical properties in studying the interior of the Earth and its satellite, particularly to depths of tens or hundreds of kilometers. At such depths, pressures and temperatures are very great, and laboratory studies in which these pressures and temperatures have been used to predict the electrical properties at depth. More direct measurements of the electrical properties deep within the earth have been made by using surface-based electrical surveys of various sorts. An important side aspect of the study of electrical properties has been the observation that, when pressures near the crushing strength are applied to a rock, marked changes in electrical properties occur, probably caused by the development of incipient fractures. Such changes in resistivity might be used in predicting earthquakes, if they can be measured in the ground. Two properties are of primary concern in the application of electrical methods:

1. The ability of rocks to conduct an electrical current-Electrical Conductivity.
2. The polarization which occurs when an electrical current is passed through them.

Electrical properties (Robert, 1988) come in two basic types: one that describes energy dissipation and the other that describes energy storage. Electrical dissipation comes as the result of charge motion (or transport), called conduction. Electrical conductivity is the ability of a material to transport charge through the process of conduction, normalized by geometry to describe a material property. Dissipation (or energy loss) results from the conversion of electrical energy to thermal energy (Joule heating) through momentum transfer during collisions as the charges move. Electrical storage is the result of charge storing energy when the application of an external force moves the charge from some equilibrium position and there is a restoring force trying to move the charge back. This process is dielectric polarization, normalized by geometry to be the material property called dielectric permittivity. As polarization occurs, causing charges to move, the charge motion is also dissipative.

4.2 Definition

4.2.1 *Electrical Resistivity*

Electrical resistivity (also known as specific electrical resistance or volume resistivity) is a measure of how strongly a material opposes the flow of electric current. A low resistivity indicates a material that readily allows the movement of electrical charge. The SI unit of electrical resistivity is the ohm meter (Ω m). The electrical resistivity ρ can be given by,

$$\rho = RA/l \qquad \dots (4.1)$$

Where 'R' is the electrical resistance of a uniform specimen of the material (measured in ohms, Ω), 'l' is the length of the piece of material (measured in meters, m); A is the cross- sectional area of the specimen (measured in square meters, m^2).

Finally, electrical resistivity is also defined as the inverse of the conductivity σ (sigma), of the material,

$$\rho = 1/\sigma \quad \ldots (4.2)$$

Resistivity (or conductivity), which governs the amount of current that passes when a potential difference is created and the unit of electrical conductivity is 1/Ohm m = $Ohm^{-1}m^{-1}$.

4.2.2 *Electrical Polarization*

Electrical polarization is the result of a wide variety of processes, including polarization of electrons in orbits around atoms, distortion of molecules, reorientation of polar molecules (like water molecules), accumulation of charge at interfaces, and electrochemical reactions. Nearly all polarization of importance in earth materials is the result of some interaction involving water. The dominant mechanisms of electrical conduction are ionic charge transport through water filling pore spaces in rocks and soils. Electrochemical activity or polarizability is the response of certain minerals to electrolytes in the ground, the bases for Self Potential and Induced Potential (Bodmer *et al.*, 1968).

4.2.3 *Dielectric Constant or Permittivity* (ε)

It is a measure of the capacity of a material to store charge when an electric field is applied. It measures the polarizability of a material in an electric field. It is defined as:

$\varepsilon = 1 + 4\pi X$, where X is the electrical susceptibility.

4.3 Electrical Conductivity of Rocks

Rocks mostly are aggregates of one or more minerals, but some are composed entirely of glassy matter, or of a mixture of glass and minerals. The electrical conductivity of rock and of minerals comprising them varies over a very wide range. Some of the minerals behave as good conductors like metals, while others have very high resistivities and show behavior like those of insulators. However, most of the rocks and rock forming minerals are semiconductors. It is well known presently that semiconductors are nearly insulators at low temperatures. At high temperatures electrical resistivity of most metals varies linearly with temperature, while semiconductors and insulators depict a negative exponential relationship between temperature and resistivity i.e., with the increase in temperature the electrical resistivity decreases.

The earth is a great reservoir of heat and the temperature inside it. Below a top layer of around 20 m thick at which the annual surface temperature wave gets greatly attenuated, temperature continuously increases with depth. There are no direct ways to determine temperatures in the earth's interior, except through measurements in boreholes drilled for exploration purposes to various depths, depending upon the need and the available technology. Considering the variation of the electrical conductivity of materials with temperature, the idea to obtain information about the thermal state and temperature distribution of the outer few hundred kilometers of the earth through the knowledge of the earth's electrical conductivity profile derived from geomagnetic variations, germinated in the minds of the scientists long back. However such efforts also needed knowledge of the electrical conductivity of earth's crustal and upper mantle materials under various temperature and pressure conditions. It has been Coster who in 1948 initiated such experiments for the first time. Through his laboratory measurements on electrical conductivity on rocks at high temperatures, he showed an exponential variation of electrical conductivity with temperature. During 1950, Bullard by using some of the experimental results of Coster (1948) and his theory of Westward drift of secular variation of geomagnetic field made the first estimate of the electrical conductivity of the earth's interior.

Since the efforts of Coster (1948) attempts have continued, in various laboratories of the world, towards studying the electrical conductivity of rocks under various temperature and pressure conditions. On the basis of his studies of the effect of pressure on the electrical conductivity of period (a mineral in upper mantle's rock—peridotits) at different temperatures, Hughes (1955) observed that the percent change of electrical conductivity with pressure can be taken as negligible. He further obtained that the total change in conductivity with pressure up to 8.5 kilo bar was about 20% and equal to that produced by a temperature change of 14°C. The electrical resistivity ($1/\sigma$) of some of the earth materials are shown in Table 4.1.

Table 4.1: The Electrical Resistivity of Various Earth's Materials

Material	*Resistivity (Ohm-meter)*
Air	Infinite
Pyrite	3×10^{-1}
Galena	2×10^{-3}
Quartz	$4 \times 10^{10} - 2 \times 10^{14}$
Calcite	$1 \times 10^{12} - 1 \times 10^{13}$
Rock Salt	$30 - 1 \times 10^{13}$
Mica	$9 \times 10^{12} - 1 \times 10^{14}$
Granite	$100 - 1 \times 10^{6}$
Gabbro	$1 \times 10^{3} - 1 \times 10^{6}$
Basalt	$10 - 1 \times 10^{7}$
Limestones	$50 - 1 \times 10^{7}$
Sandstones	$1 - 1 \times 10^{8}$
Shales	$20 - 2 \times 10^{3}$
Dolomite	100 – 10,000
Sand	1 – 1,000
Clay	1 – 100
Ground Water	0.5 – 300
Sea Water	0.2

4.4 Electrical Conduction in Rocks

The rocks and their minerals belong to one or the other group of solids. Their electrical conductivities vary over a much wider range than any other of their physical properties i.e., thermal conductivity, porosity, density, compressional wave velocities, etc. Some of the minerals are metallic while some other have very high resistivity and behave like insulators (Keller, 1966). However, most of the rocks and rock forming minerals are semiconductors. By assuming isotropic material, electrical conductivity 'σ' becomes a scalar quantity and in case of anisotropic material, it is a tensor quality.

In pure semiconductors, the external low electric field can not provide that much of activation energy to cross the forbidden gap. Therefore, inter zone transfer of electrons from valence band to conduction band can be excited by thermal process of impurity atoms.

The electrical conductivity of a semiconductor is highly sensitive to even minor variations in the chemical composition. Impurities, not only the foreign atoms in the chemical composition as well as various defects in the crystal lattice, serve as the source of charge carriers. Therefore impurity plays a most important role at low temperatures while at high temperatures electrical conduction is mainly a thermally activated process.

The influence of impurity is so large on electrical conductivity of rocks and minerals that often the same mineral collected from different sources does not give the same electrical conductivity. The range may be as large as two or three orders of magnitude. The type of impurity may lead to one type of conduction in one sample, and to the another type in the other sample.

The electrical conductivity of rocks depends upon various parameters viz., pressure, temperature, mineral composition, liquid content, shape and size of mineral grains, texture, etc.

at high temperature, only temperature effect is significant as compared to other parameters. The relationship can be described as,

$$\sigma_t = \sum \sigma_{0i} \exp(-E_i/K_B T) \quad \ldots (4.3)$$

Where, E_i is the activation energy, which depends upon conduction mechanism, K_B is Boltzmann's constant and σ_{0i} is a constant, may be called as initial conductivity of each species. As most of the rock and rock forming minerals behave like semiconductors, a detailed theory of electrical conduction in semiconductors is well discussed by Gupta and Kumar (1976).

4.5 Calculation of Activation Energy (E_i)

Let σ_1 and σ_2 be the electrical conductivities of the specimen at absolute temperatures T_1 and T_2 respectively. Solving the equation 4.3 and putting the value of Boltmann's constant (K_B) of 1.38×10^{-16} ergs/deg, the activation energy for intrinsic or impurity conduction (Gupta and Sharma, 1978),

$$E_i = 0.4 \text{ Tan } \theta \; ev \quad \ldots (4.4)$$

Where slop of the line between 1000/T and $\text{Log}_{10}\sigma$,

$$\text{Tan } \theta = \text{Log}_{10}\sigma_2 - \text{Log}_{10}\sigma_1/(1000/T_2) - (1000/T_1) \quad \ldots (4.5)$$

and $1 \; e\,v = 1.6 \times 10^{-12}$ ergs

Similarly for ionic conduction where,

$$\sigma i = \sigma_{01} \, e^{-Ei/K_B T} \quad \ldots (4.6)$$

and activation energy can be calculated by using,

$$E_i = 0.2 \text{ Tan } \theta \quad \ldots (4.7)$$

4.6 Measurement Techniques for Electrical Resistivity

Most of the rocks and rock forming minerals are electrically semi conductors. Therefore the techniques suitable for the measurement of electrical resistivity of semiconductors in the laboratory may also be used for rocks and minerals. There are two main groups of techniques which are generally used for the determination of resistivity of semiconductors. These are:

- Direct current (d.c.) techniques and
- Alternating current (a.c.) techniques.

In both the techniques, the resistivity of the sample (ρ) is calculated by measuring the potential difference across two equipotential surfaces (V) and the current flowing through the sample (I) using the formula,

$$\rho = V.A/I.L \qquad \text{... (4.8)}$$

Where '*A*' is the cross sectional area of the sample and *L* is the spacing between potential electrodes.

The d.c. techniques are most commonly used. These are further broadly classified as i) two electrodes technique, and ii) four electrodes technique. The primary consideration of using d.c. techniques are to minimize the contact resistance between the sample surfaces and electrodes and polarization effect. Therefore, in these techniques the choice of electrodes' material and the conducting substance in between sample's surfaces and the surfaces of electrodes are very important. At room temperature, graphite, lead electrodes can be used. Gold and platinum electrodes deposited on the samples give very good results. The contact resistance between the sample and the electrodes can be minimized by using metal foil or sheet in between them. Using conductive silver cement with silver foils or sheets give very good results. Sometimes mercury is also used to ensure good contacts with rock sample. At elevated temperatures (up to 1100 K), silver, gold and or platinum electrodes with conductive paints over the surface of the samples are most suitable. The details of the measurement techniques of electrical resistivity at room temperature, at elevated temperatures (≈1100 K), and up to 375 K for saturated samples under pressure-temperature conditions are well described by Gupta and Sharma (1978); Sharma (1987).

4.7 Electrical Resistivity of Saturated Rock

Electrical methods form one of the important tools for the exploration of ground water and geothermal energy resources. The results of field surveys in various geothermal fields of the world have unambiguitly shown that the electrical resistivity of the subsurface rocks constituting the geothermal reservoir (water dominated) and ground water reservoir is significantly lower than the surrounding rocks. The laboratory data of the electrical resistivity of probable reservoir and surrounding rocks help for a better interpretation of field data.

In water bearing rocks, the electrical conductivity (1/resistivity) depends on mineral contents, grain size, temperature, and the amount of fluid present. The salinity of water and the way the water is distributed through the rocks are also important. At normal temperature, the effect of water content in the pores of rock is very significant on its electrical conductivity. At elevated temperatures (>500 K), the effect of water and other physical parameters become negligible, that is the contribution of temperature and mineral conductivity become important than of pore fluid conductivity.

Chinh (2000) studied the electrical properties of sedimentary rocks having interconnected water-saturated pore spaces and influence of pore fluid resistivity and bulk surface conduction on rock resistivity. The rock resistivity of all samples increased with increasing pore fluid resistivity, however, it became almost constant at a point. Sharma (1982) measured the electrical resistivity of the Deccan basalts from different hot spring and earthquake prone areas in different physical conditions i.e. dry, normal and saturated conditions at normal pressure conditions

(NTP). The values at dry state are of the order of 10^5 to 10^6 Ohm m, at normal room condition, electrical resistivity ranges from 10^2 to 10^4 Ohm m, and under saturated condition, from 10^2 to 10^3 Ohm m. The large variation in resistivity from dry to normal and saturated condition indicates that the moisture filled in pore space and fluid conductivity plays the significant role in conduction along with the conduction by minerals.

Using the measured values of electrical d.c. resistivity of brine-saturated cores from a wide variety of sand stone formations, Archie (1942) formulated an empirical relation for the bulk resistivity,

$$\rho = \rho_w \Phi^{-m} \qquad \dots (4.9)$$

Where 'ρ_w' is the resistivity of water as it actually exists in the pore space and Φ is the porosity. The exponent 'm' is the cementation index. Numerous studies (Chinh, 2000) and other references there in) have reconfirmed Archie's finding for clay free sedimentary rocks and even for igneous rocks with the cementation index 'm' ranging between certain limits,

$$1.3 \leq m \leq 4 \qquad \dots (4.10)$$

Some of the scientists (Keller, 1967) feel that Archie's relationship is better expressed by introducing an empirical parameter, 'a' as,

$$\rho = a\,\rho_w \Phi^{-m} \qquad \dots (4.11)$$

The value of 'a' varies from less than 1 for rocks with intergrannular porosity to slightly more than 1 for rocks of joint porosity.

4.8 Electrical Conductivity of Rocks at Elevated Temperatures

The electrical conductivity of rocks at elevated temperatures is most useful to investigate the physical state of the deep earth's interior and for the behavioral study of rocks. It is studied globally by various scientists (Hughes, 1955; Bradeley *et al.*, 1964, Mizutani and Kanamori, 1967; Watenbe, 1970; Dvorak, 1973; Duba *et al.*, 1974; Vorbyevv *et al.*, 1975; Stiller *et al.*, 1976; Gupta and Sharma, 1978; Sharma *et al.*, 1987; Marcela *et al.*, 1987; Stefan *et al.*, 2000; Wang Doujum *et al.*, 2002; Scarlato *et al.*, 2004; Maoschuang *et al.*, 2008. Uyeda and Rikitake(1970), in their discussion of the relationship between terrestrial heat flow and electrical conductivity anomalies observed in the earth's interior argue that although, in general, the conductivity depends upon temperature, pressure, bulk composition, presence of impurities and particularly on water. The effect of temperature predominates over that of other factors at deeper depth. They further pointed out that the effect of pressure is normally disregarded except at depth where pressure induced phase transitions might occur. The percentage change in electrical conductivity with pressure is much less as compared to the change with temperature (Hughes, 1955; Bradley *et al.*, 1964; Dvorak, 1973, Mostafa *et al.*, 2003).

Brace (1971), while discussing the resistivity of saturated rocks to 40km based on lab. data, points out that the conductivity–temperature curves for dry rocks probably can be applied to saturated rocks at high temperature, as above few hundred degrees, mineral conduction dominates over the conduction through pore fluids. Gupta and Sharma (1978); Sharma (1982); Sharma *et al.* (1987) measured the electrical conductivity of various crustal and upper mantle rocks in the temperature range between 450 to 1100 K in Argon environment and at one atmosphere pressure. Increase of electrical conductivity with increase in temperature has been observed in all the samples of granite (Figure 4.1), Basalts (Figure 4.2), except one of the sample of charnockite (Figure 4.3), Dunite and all the samples of serpentinite (Figure 4.4). However few

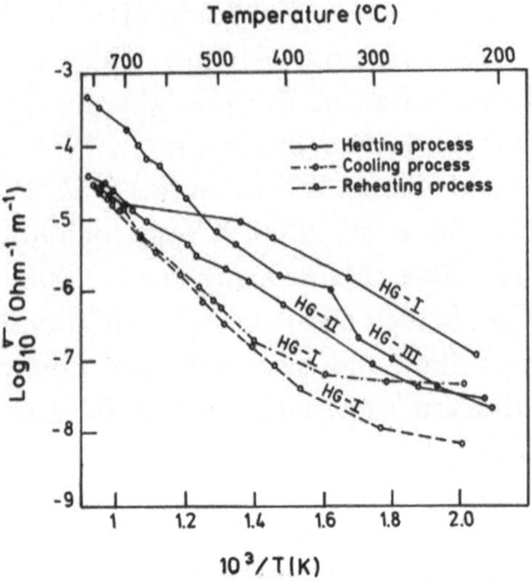

Fig. 4.1: Relationship between Electrical Conductivity and Reciprocal of Absolute Temperature for some Acidic Rocks (Granite) from Honanali Area, Southern Indian Shield (Sharma *et al.*, 1987)

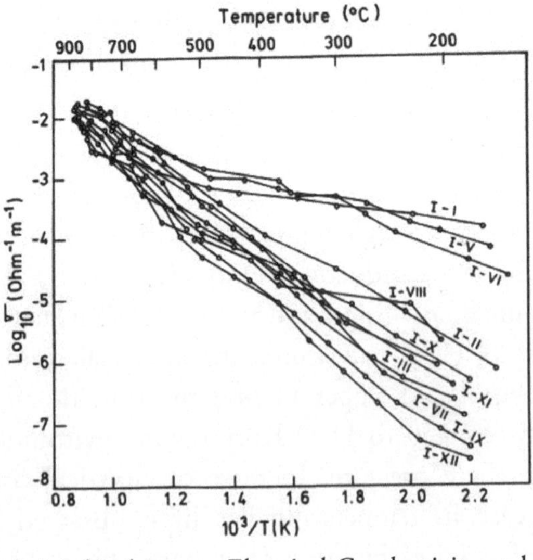

Fig. 4.2: Relationship between Electrical Conductivity and Reciprocal of Absolute Temperature for some Basalt from Igatpuri Area, Deccan Trap, India (Sharma *et al.*, 1987)

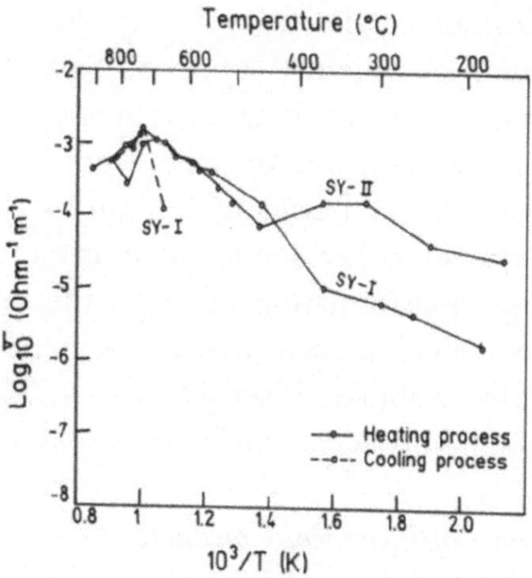

Fig. 4.3: Relationship between Electrical Conductivity and Reciprocal of Absolute Temperature for some Intermediate Rocks (Charnokite) from Salem Area, Southern Indian Shield (Sharma *et al.*, 1987)

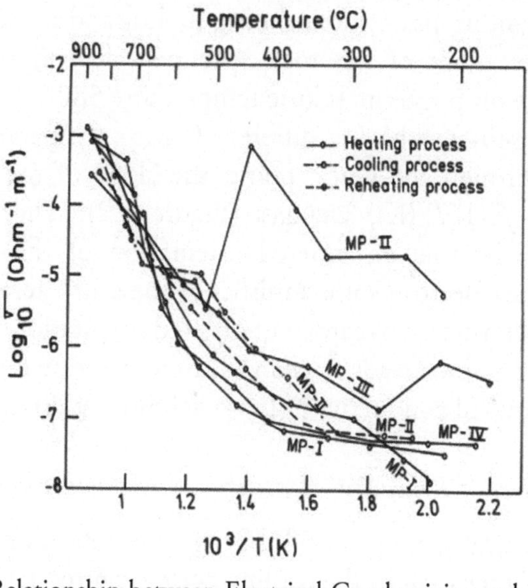

Fig. 4.4: Relationship between Electrical Conductivity and Reciprocal of Absolute Temperature for some Ultramafic Rocks (Peridotite, Dunite) from Drass Area, Himalaya, India (Sharma *et al.*, 1987)

samples of Deccan basalts from Pawagarh areas have also shown anomalous behaviour (Gupta and Sharma, 1978).The anomalous behaviour in electrical conductivity variation with temperature in the temperature range from 600–1000 K as observed in some of the basalts of Deccan basalts and upper mantle rocks may be either due to the transformation of Fe^{+2} to Fe^{+3} ions i.e. transformation of magnetite in to hematite mineral and/or dehydration of hydrous mineral components (Noritomi, 1961; Zabloki, 1964; Dvorak, 1973; Gupta and Sharma, 1978; Sharma *et al.*, 1987).

4.8.1 *Behaviour of Electrical Conductivity of Deccan Basalts at Curie Point*

Electrical conductivity of basalts depends upon magnetic minerals. The composition of magnetic minerals in basaltic rocks is governed by the composition of parent magma and physical conditions operative during cooling and crystallization. The Curie point of the rock specimen depends upon the percentage of magnetite (Curie temperature 580°C) and other magnetic minerals having different Curie's temperatures. On passing through the Curie point, the slope of the function $\mathrm{Log}_{10}\sigma = f\,(1/T\ (\mathrm{K}))$ changes (Figure 4.2). The exchange energy, generating an ordered orientation of the magnetic moments of electron spins vanishes at the Curie temperatures and temperatures above it, an unordered orientation of spins is established, which leads to change in temperature dependence of the electrical conductivity (Lastovickova, 1978).

4.8.2 *Effect of Repeating Heating on Conductivity*

The electrical conductivity during the reheating cycle is slightly higher than in the cooling cycle (Figures 4.1 and 4.4). This behavior has been reported by various authors (Schober, 1971; Duba, 1972; Dvorak, 1973; Gupta and Sharma, 1978; Sharma *et al.*, 1987). The change in electrical conductivity with repeated heating might be due to an increase in the number of charge carriers due to heat treatment. However, a change of surface, grain boundary, conductivity may be considered as another or additional explanation (Gupta and Sharma, 1978).

4.9 Applications

4.9.1 *Electrical Conductivity Structure of the Earth's Interior*

Attempts to estimate the electrical conductivity of the earth's crust by using laboratory data on electrical conductivity of crustal rocks have been made by Noritomi (1961); Caner, 1970; Sharma *et al.*, 1987). The main problem in giving the conductivity structure in the earth's interior while using the laboratory data, is the knowledge of temperature distribution within the earth. Based on heat flow and heat generation studies, using various geothermal models, temperatures inside the earth can be estimated and then electrical structure of the earth's interior up to upper mantle can be obtained (Uyeda and Rikitake 1970). Specifically for the southern Indian Shield, electrical conductivity structure using heat flow data and laboratory data of electrical conductivity of rocks has been suggested by Sharma *et al.* (1987). They suggested that beneath southern Indian Shield, the value of electrical conductivity at 20km depth is of the order of 10^{-8} mhos/m and at Mohorovicic discontinuity; it is of the order of 10^{-4} mhos/m.

4.9.2 *Temperature Distribution in the Upper Mantle*

Using vertical electrical conductivity distribution inferred from long period electromagnetic (EM) field data, the teleseismic signals of *P* and *S* waves and laboratory data of electrical conductivity of crustal and upper mantle rocks, the temperature distribution in the upper mantle can be found out (Sharma and Veeraswami, 1998).

CHAPTER V

Seismic Properties

5.1 Introduction

During the past 50 years or so, tremendous progress has been made in studying physical properties of rocks and minerals in relation to seismic exploration and earthquake seismology. During the early years of exploration seismology, seismic data were interpreted primarily for structures that might trap hydrocarbons. With the advancement of computing power and seismic processing and interpretation techniques, seismic data are now commonly analyzed for determining lithology, porosity, pore fluids, and saturation.

Seismic properties are affected in complex ways by many factors, such as pressure, temperature, saturation, fluid type, porosity, pore type, etc. These factors are often interrelated or coupled in a way that many also change when one factor changes. The effect of these changes on seismic data can be either additive or subtractive. As a result, investigation of the effect of varying a single parameter while fixing others becomes imperative in understanding rock physics applications to seismic interpretations.

The seismic properties of rocks are usually thought of in terms of Compressional (*P*) wave velocity—V_p and Shear (*S*) wave velocity—V_s, which are both functions of density, porosity, pressure and temperature, etc. Knowledge of high-pressure-temperature laboratory measurements of seismic velocity for a wide range of rocks that are commonly found in the crust with the results of seismic refraction profiles can be used to infer crustal composition as a function of depth and a great deal about the composition and physical state of materials in the earth (Christensen and Mooney, 1995). The earth is, however, much more complex than this simple approach would indicate. Seismic surveys yield maps of the distribution of seismic velocities, interfaces between rocks units and ideally of reflection coefficients at these interfaces. The velocities of some of the earth materials which vary widely are shown in Table 5.1.

Table 5.1: The P- and S-Wave Velocities of Various Earth Materials (G - Gebrande *et al.*, 1982; S - Schon, 1996)

Material	*P Wave Velocity, Km/sec*	*S Wave Velocity, Km/sec*	*Reference*
Air	0.332		
Water	14–1.5		
Petroleum	1.3–1.4		
Concrete	3.60	2.0	
Granite	4.18–5.85	2.61–3.30	G
Basalt	4.67–6.15	2.61–3.51	S
Sandstone	1.4–4.3	0.7–2.8	S
Saturated shale	1.5–2.0	0.5–0.75	G
Limestone	5.9–6.1	2.8–3.0	G
Dolomite	3.5–6.50	1.9–3.60	S
Sand (Unsaturated)	0.2–1.0	0.80–0.40	S
Sand (Saturated)	0.800–2.2	0.32–0.880	S
Clay	1.0–2.5	0.4–1.0	S
Diorite	4.83–6.37	2.96–3.35	S
Gabbro	5.99–6.93	3.31–3.69	S
Andesite	3.97–6.13	2.44–3.50	S
Gneiss	5.00–6.35	2.55–3.55	S
Quartzite	2.46–5.56	1.79–1.33	S
Serpentinite	4.25–6.23	2.07–3.49	G
Granulite	5.36–6.50	3.10–3.57	S
Eclogite	6.53–8.01	3.56–4.56	G

Seismologists desire to measure physical properties to the greatest level of detail possible. Their aim is to determine not only the composition of the earth but also its physical state. The question of composition is complex because rocks are combinations of minerals which each have their own seismic properties. In general, the velocities of the crystalline rocks which constitute most of the earth's lithosphere are inversely proportional to the silicon dioxide content and directly proportional to the content of iron and magnesium oxides.

Many factors, such as porosity, pressure, and temperature, affect the seismic velocity of a particular rock. Table 5.1 shows that the unconsolidated sediments (sand) can have very low velocities. Clastic sedimentary rocks (sandstone and shale) are 'slower' than carbonate sedimentary rocks (limestone and dolomite). For typical crystalline rocks, granite (felsic) is slower than gabbro (mafic), which is slower than granulite (ultramafic). These relationships are generally reflected in the velocity structure of the Earth's lithosphere, in which the granitic upper crust generally has higher velocities than the sedimentary rocks which cover it but has lower velocities than the more mafic lower crust. The ultramafic mantle, which is very rich in iron, has even higher velocities.

5.2 Definitions

There are many different seismic waves, but all of basically of four types:

- Compressional or P (for primary) wave
- Transverse or S (for secondary) wave
- Love wave
- Rayleigh wave.

5.2.1 *Compressional Wave (P-wave)*

A wave in which the disturbance is a compression of the medium is called Compressional Wave (P-wave). Compressional waves are also called 'longitudinal waves'. Compressional waves move straight in one direction parallel to the medium. These are also called primary waves. In primary waves, the energy propagates by change in volume (compression/dilation). P-waves are sound waves, it's just that in seismology the scientists are interested in frequencies that are lower than humans' range of hearing (the speed of sound in air is about 0.3 km/sec). The vibration caused by P-waves is a volume change, alternating from compression to expansion in the direction that the wave is traveling. P-waves travel through all types of media—solid, liquid, or gas.

5.2.2 *Shear Wave (S-wave)*

A wave in which the disturbance is an elastic deformation perpendicular to the direction of motion of the wave is called Shear Wave (S-wave). Shear waves are also called 'transverse waves.' Shear waves move side to side, only move through solids, and are also called secondary waves. These are slower than compressional waves, travel perpendicular to the medium. In S-waves, the energy propagates by change of shape which is not possible in fluids. An important distinguishing characteristic of an S-wave is its inability to propagate through a fluid or a gas because a fluids and gasses cannot transmit a shear stress and S-waves are waves that shear the material.

In general, earthquakes generate larger shear waves than compressional waves and much of the damage close to an earthquake is the result of strong shaking caused by shear waves. Generally, the seismic velocities depend on the elastic moduli and density. The relationship, in a homogeneous and isotropic media, can be expressed as,

$$V_P = \sqrt{(K + 4/3\mu)/\rho} \quad \text{... (5.1)}$$

$$V_s = \sqrt{\mu/\rho} \quad \text{... (5.2)}$$

Where elastic constants, K and μ are the Bulk and Shear moduli of the media. ρ is the density of the material. These elastic constants, and densities depend on the properties that the geologist or engineer use to characterise the rock such as porosity, fluid saturation, texture, etc. A review of the relationships between the intrinsic rock properties and the measured velocities is needed before seismic survey results can be interpreted quantitatively in terms of lithology. Many of these relationships are empirical. Velocities are found to be related to certain rock units in a given locale by actual laboratory measurements on core sample of the rock or soil.

5.2.3 *Love Waves*

Love waves are transverse waves that vibrate the ground in the horizontal direction perpendicular to the direction that the waves are traveling. They are formed by the interaction of S-waves with earth's surface and shallow structure and are dispersive waves. The speed at which a dispersive wave travels depends on the wave's period. In general, earthquakes generate Love waves over a range of periods from 1000 to a fraction of a second, and each period travels at a different velocity but the typical range of velocities is between 2 and 6 km/second. Another important characteristic of Love waves is that the amplitude of ground vibration caused by a Love wave decreases with depth. Like the velocity the rate of amplitude decrease with depth also depends on the period.

5.2.4 *Rayleigh Waves*

Rayleigh waves are the slowest of all the seismic wave types and in some ways the most complicated. Like Love waves they are dispersive so the particular speed at which they travel depends on the wave period and the near-surface geologic structure, and they also decrease in amplitude with depth. Typical speeds for Rayleigh waves are on the order of 1 to 5 km/s.

Seismic waves can be distinguished by a number of properties including the speed the waves travel, the direction that the waves move particles as they pass by, where and where they don't propagate. The first two wave types, P and S, are called body waves because they travel or propagate through the body of earth. The latter two are called surface waves they the travel along Earth's surface and their amplitude decreases with depth into earth. An earthquake radiates P and S waves in all directions and the interaction of the P and S waves with earth's surface and shallow structure produces surface waves.

Near an earthquake the shaking is large and dominated by shear-waves and short-period surface waves. These are the waves that do the most damage to our buildings, highways, etc. Even in large earthquakes the intense shaking generally lasts only a few tens of seconds, but it can last for minutes in the greatest earthquakes. At farther distances, the amplitude of the seismic wave decreases as the energy released by the earthquake spreads throughout a larger volume of earth. Also with increasing distance from the earthquake, the waves are separated apart in time and dispersed because P, S and surface waves travel at different speeds.

5.2.5 *Bulk Modulus (K)*

It is defined as the ratio of the pressure applied to the material to the amount of volume change that the material undergoes.

If '*K*' is large then the material is very stiff, meaning that it does not compress very much even undergoes large pressure. If '*K*' is small, the small pressure can compress the material by large amounts. For example, gases have very small incompressibility, solids and liquids have large compressibility.

5.2.6 *Shear Modulus (μ)*

The shear modulus (μ) describes how difficult to deform a material under an applied shearing force. If the material has a small shear modulus, it will be deformed with small shearing force. If the material has a large shear modulus, it will take a large force applied to the direction to deform the material.

5.2.7 *Modulus of Elasticity (E)*

The ratio between stress (σ) and strain (ε) is referred to as the 'Modulus of Elasticity', or Young's Modulus and is denoted as E. Mathematically:

$$E = (P/A)/(\Delta L/L) = \sigma/\varepsilon \qquad \ldots (5.3)$$

5.2.8 *Poisson's Ratio*

It is the ratio of transverse contraction strain to longitudinal extension strain in the direction of stretching force. Tensile deformation is considered positive and compressive deformation is considered negative. Poisson's ratio, also called Poisson ratio or the Poisson coefficient, is usually represented as 'ν'.

$$\nu = \varepsilon_{trans}/\varepsilon_{longitudinal} \qquad \ldots (5.4)$$

Strain ε is defined in elementary form as the change in length divided by the original length (Figure 5.1),

$$\varepsilon = \Delta L/L \qquad \ldots (5.5)$$

Poisson's ratio is related to elastic moduli—the bulk modulus

(K), the shear modulus (μ), and Young's modulus (E), by the following,

$$\nu = (3K-2\,\mu)/(6K+2\,\mu) \quad \ldots (5.6)$$

$$E = 2\,\mu\,(1+\nu) \quad \ldots (5.7)$$

The study of Poisson's ratio behaviour in various crystalline rocks under different temperatures and pressures shows this parameter to depend upon the rock composition rather than upon P–T conditions (Tarkov and Vavakin, 1982). This ratio varies in natural rock from between 0.1 to 0.5. The use of Poisson's ratio is in the analysis of the propagation of an energy wave generated by an earthquake. This wave moves through solid rock and is, therefore, somewhat subjected to rock properties. The speed of propagation, or wave velocity, is dependent upon the Poisson's ratio of the rock.

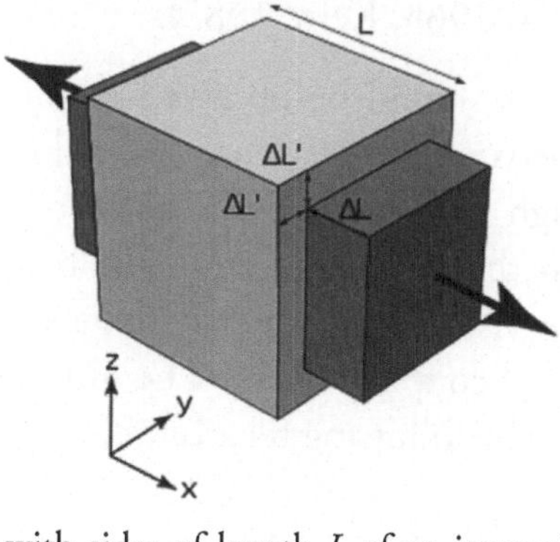

Fig. 5.1: A cube with sides of length L of an isotropic linearly elastic material subject to tension along the x axis. The green cube is unstressed, the red is expanded in the x direction by L due to tension, and contracted in the y and z directions by L'.

5.3 Measurement Techniques for Seismic Velocities

The seismic velocities (P- and S-waves) in laboratory are measured with the Non destructive ultrasonic method. This method is based on the propagation of an ultrasonic wave form from a transmitter to a receiver. The waves can be emitted continuously or in a pulse mode. Compressional (P) and Shear (S) waves were generated by means of transducers. Transmitting and receiving transducers were mounted at the opposing ends of the cylindrical samples. P-Wave and the S-Wave measurements were made on the cores in longitudinal mode. The piezoelectric ceramics (2.54 cm diameter, 1-MHz frequency, P-wave transducers or 18 × 18 mm size, 1-MHz frequency, S-wave transducers) were placed at both ends of the cores for the P- and S-wave measurements, respectively. The S- wave ceramics provide a mechanical pulse polarized parallel to the ends of the samples and care need to be taken to ensure that the polarization directions of both transverse mode ceramics were properly aligned to each other and appropriately oriented with respect to the rock's principal textural *X*-, *Y*-, *Z*-axes (Simmons, 1965; Kern, 1982).

Some precautions should be observed in ultrasonic method. Acoustical impedance of the sensors should match with the material through the use of the correct coupling media. Water has been the best coupling media because of its ready availability, low viscosity. A water-based gel has proven to be the most practical coupling agent. The ultrasonic velocity was measured using the following relation,

$$V = d/\Delta t \qquad \ldots (5.8)$$

Knowing the sample thickness (d) in micron resolution and transit time (Δt) in Nano-second resolution, the overall accuracy obtained in the measurement of velocity is ± 5 ms^{-1} (Rajendran *et al.*, 2002).

This method has been used by scientists and modified accordingly depending upon the needs of the problems (Simmons, 1965; Fielitz, 1971); Bayuk and Tedeyev, 1974; Spencer and Nur,

1976; Steward and Peselnick, 1977; Ramananantoandro and Manghnani,1978; Kern, 1982; Castagna *et al.*, 1985; Zamora *et al.*, 1994; Jason *et al.*, 2004. This technique is also modified for the measurement of P and S wave velocities in crustal and mantle rocks under the high pressure and temperature (Kern, 1982 and other references there in; Phillips *et al.*, 1989; Kern and Tubia, 1993; Khazanehdari *et al.*, 2000).

5.4 Rock Properties that Affect Seismic Velocity and Empirical Relationship

The results on seismic velocities affected by various rock properties can be used for better seismic analysis performance, correspond to increase hydrocarbon discovery from the carbonate rocks. These data are used to interpret the seismic velocity structure of the interior of the earth. Interval transit time data derived from seismic velocities are useful to predict clay mineralogy and overpressures from compaction trends for hydrocarbon exploration. The relationship between the seismic velocities and other rock properties becomes very useful when independent information on one of properties is available.. These relationships are only approximate. One should not lose sight of the fact that many types of rocks share the same P-wave velocity, V_p (Table 5.1). More independent measurements of other seismic properties are thus highly desirable so that the type of rock and its physical state can be better determined. Empirical relationships among seismic velocity, effective pressure, porosity and clay content in sand stone is given by Phillips *et al.* (1989).

5.4.1 *Porosity and Permeability*

The porosity and permeability are the main factor in determining acoustic wave velocity in carbonate rocks. An increase in porosity and permeability will decrease in velocity both compressional and shear waves. A very rough rule due to Wyllie *et al.* (1956) is the so called time average relationship:

$$\frac{1}{V_{\text{bulk}}} = \frac{\Phi}{V_{\text{fluid}}} + \frac{1-\Phi}{V_{\text{matrix}}} \qquad \dots (5.9)$$

Where Φ is the porosity.

This is not based on any convincing theory but is roughly right when the effective pressure is high and the rock is fully saturated.

Velocity is strongly dependent on the rock-porosity. Compressional wave velocity (Vp) decreases inversely with porosity (Wang and Noor, 1992). An increase in porosity from (5% to 20%) will resulting a decrease in velocity from 4500 m/s to 2000 m/s. Increasing porosity will create a mount of pore space that cause slow of acoustic velocity (Schon, 1996). For the shear wave velocity (Vs), an increase in porosity (5% to 20%) will result a decrease in velocity (2300 m/s to 1000 m/s). Porosity (percentage of pore space) is particularly important in the sedimentary rocks found near the earth's surface. Burial at depth, giving rise to high overburden pressures, causes sedimentary rocks in particular to compact. In the process, their porosity decreases and their seismic velocity increases correspondingly.

The same phenomenon also occurs in the correlation between permeability and acoustic wave velocities. An increase in permeability (1.8 mD to 10.2 mD) will cause a decrease in compressional wave velocity (Vp) from 4600 m/s to 2000 m/s. For the shear wave velocity (Vs), there is also a clear inverse trend; an increase in permeability (5% to 20%) will caused a decrease in velocity from 2300 mD to 1000 mD (MacKay *et al.*, 1995).

5.4.2 *Lithification*

It is also known as cementation. The degree, to which grains in a sedimentary rock are cemented together by post depositional, usually chemical, processes, has a strong effect on the modulii. By filling pore space with minerals of higher density than the fluid it replaces the bulk density is also increased. The combination of porosity reduction and lithification cause the observed increase of velocity with depth of burial and age (Karner *et al.*, 1997; Behn and Kelemen, 2003).

5.4.3 *Density*

The correlation between seismic *P*-wave velocity and density (ρ) has been proved by numerous laboratory investigations of elastic properties of crustal rocks (Stanley *et al.*, 2003). Seismic velocities increase linearly with the increase in density of rocks. However one of the problems connected with this approach is that rocks with high content of calcium-reach plagioclase have higher *P*-wave velocity and do not satisfy the common density-*Vp* relationship (Kozlovskaya *et al.*, 2004). Birch (1961) suggested the empirical relationship between V_p and density (ρ) as,

$$V_p = a + b\,\rho \qquad \text{... (5.10)}$$

Where '*a*' and '*b*' are the empirical parameters. He found for magmatic rocks the relation,

$$V_p = 2.76\,\rho - 0.98 \qquad \text{... (5.11)}$$

His samples were from North American continent and India. These parameters (*a* and *b*) vary according to the type of rocks (Schon, 1996). However, Compressional wave velocities are only roughly related to densities (Kern, 1982). He observed three distinct areas. Possible upper mantle rocks are characterized by high velocities and high densities. Tholeitic basalts, possible representative of the oceanic crust, exhibit relatively low compressional wave velocities and high densities. Plutonic and metamorphic acidic and basic rocks have in general relatively high mean velocities in respect to their densities.

In general, high contents of high density minerals—olivine, garnet, pyroxene and amphibole produce high compressional and shear wave velocities and relatively high Poisson's ratios. Increasing quartz content results in a decrease of *Vp* and accompanying increase in *Vs*, there by significantly lowering the Poisson's ratio (Kern, 1978, 1982).

5.4.4 *Pressure*

The rocks exhibit an increase in velocity with increasing pressure, as micro-cracks in the rock close, reducing their porosity. Compressional wave velocity is strongly dependant on effective stress. Velocity drastically increases with pressure (3650 m/s to 3900 m/s) in the low pressure range (50 to 200 bar), because the thinnest pores close at low pressures and the compacted rocks will have higher acoustic velocity. Further increasing of pressure in the higher pressure range has less effect on the velocities because cracks may have already been closed (Birch, 1960). The effect of overburden pressure to the shear wave velocity is relatively similar to compressional wave velocity. The shear velocity drastically increases (1840 m/s to 1940 m/s) even in the lower pressure range (50 to 200 bar). At higher pressure range, the velocities increase is less.

For a rock buried in the earth the confining pressure is the pressure of the overlying rock column, the pore water pressure may be the hydrostatic pressure if there is connected porosity to the surface or it may be greater or less than hydrostatic. The effective pressure is the difference between the confining and pore pressure.

In general velocity rises with increasing confining pressure and then levels off to a "terminal velocity" when the effective pressure is high (Birch, 1960, 61; Kern and Tubia, 1993). The effect is probably due to crack closure. At low effective pressure cracks are open and easily closed with an increase in stress. As the effective pressure increases the cracks are all closed, Bulk modulus '*K*' goes up and the velocity increases.

Finally even at depth, as the pore pressure increases above hydrostatic, the effective pressure decreases as does the velocity. Over pressured zones can be detected in a sedimentary sequence by their anomalously low velocities. Increasing age also causes the velocity of sedimentary rocks to increase because many processes that take place in the earth tend to decrease the porosity. Crystalline rocks also exhibit an increase in velocity with increasing pressure, as micro-cracks in the rock close, reducing their porosity. In the mantle, phase transformations of olivine result in more compact crystal structures which are believed to cause the seismic discontinuities that are consistently observed at several depths on a global basis.

5.4.5 *Temperature*

Temperature is another factor that affects the seismic properties of rocks. If other factors are held constant, an increase in temperature generally causes a decrease in seismic velocity, but the rate varies from rock type to rock type and depends strongly on the confining pressure operating on the polycrystalline material (Kern, 1982). Since temperature increases with depth in the earth, we might expect seismic velocity to decrease with depth. Except in small regions, this is not, because in general the temperature effect is offset by the effects of pressure and composition (Kern and Richter, 1981; Kern and Tubia 1993, Ito and Tatsumi, 1995).

The speed depends on the rock type because it allows using observations recorded on seismograms to infer the composition or range of compositions of the planet. But the process isn't always simple, because sometimes different rock types have the same seismic-wave velocity, and other factors also affect the speed, particularly temperature and pressure. Temperature tends to lower the speed of seismic waves and pressure tends to increase the speed. Pressure increases with depth in earth because the weight of the rocks above gets larger with increasing depth. Usually, the effect of pressure is the larger and in regions of uniform composition, the velocity generally increases with depth, despite the fact that the increase of temperature with depth works to lower the wave velocity confining pressure (Lin, and Wang, 1980; Khazanehdari *et al.*, 2000).

The temperature derivatives refer to 20–500°C at 6 kbar, for plutonic and metamorphic rocks range from –0.72 to -8.19×10^{-4} km/s°C for compressional wave velocities and from –1.39 to -4.53×10^{-4} km/s°C for Shear wave velocities (Kern, 1982). Under simultaneous action of temperature and high confining pressure, however, cracks and pore spaces are closed effectively, giving rise to the observed significantly low velocity decrease or even increase in the basalts with increasing temperature. The reasons for the abrupt velocity decrease around 350°C in basalts containing hydrous zeolite minerals. Part or all water is given off continuously or abruptly on heating from room temperature to about 350°C. Dehydration reactions of zeolite minerals may account for the anomalous velocity behaviour (Kern, 1982).

The ultrasonic measurements of *Vp* and *Vs* as a function of temperature at constant confining pressure indicate an anomalous behavior of wave velocities in quartz bearing rocks like granite, gneiss and quartzite at temperatures(≈573°C) at which the high-low transition in the constituent quartz crystals is expected. The α–β quartz transition is associated with a pronounced decrease in velocity of compressional wave velocity when approaching the transition, and with a significant velocity increase after the transition. In contrast, the effect of high-low transition on shear wave velocities is small (Kern, 1982).

5.4.6 *Fluid Saturation*

From theoretical and empirical studies it is found that the compressional wave velocity decreases with decreasing fluid saturation. As the fraction of gas in the pores increases '*K*' and hence velocity decreases. Less intuitive is the fact that V_s also decreases with an increase in gas content. The reflection coefficient is strongly affected if one of the contacting media is gas saturated because the impedance is lowered by both the density and velocity decreases.

Measurements of dry velocity versus pressure and porosity versus pressure contain all of the necessary information for predicting the frequency-dependent effects of fluid saturation. Furthermore, these measurements automatically incorporate all pore interaction, so there is no limitation to low crack density. The velocities are found to depend on five key interrelated variables: frequency, the distribution of compliant crack-like porosity, the intrinsic or non-crack anisotropy, fluid viscosity and compressibility, and effective pressure. The sensitivity of velocities to saturation is generally greater at high frequencies than low frequencies (Mukerji and Mavko, 1994).

5.5 Relationship with Other Geophysical Parameters

Seismic velocities are correlated with the other geophysical parameters like radioactive heat generation, heat flow, electrical conductivity, etc. Radioactive heat generation, compressional wave velocity and density are related to rock type in crystalline rocks (Rybach, 1976).

The empirical exponential relationship between radioactive heat production (*A*) and *P* wave velocity (*Vp*) at depth '*z*' in crustal rocks has been suggested as,

$$A(z) = a.\exp(bVp) \qquad \text{... (5.12)}$$

Where the numerical factors '*a*' and '*b*' depend upon insitu pressure (Rybach and Buntebarth, 1984). However, Fountain (1986) pointed out that heat production cannot be reliably predicted from seismic velocity. These two parameters are not likely to be related as velocity depends upon the major mineral constituents of rocks whereas heat production results from radiogenic components concentrated in both major and trace minerals in rocks.

Deep seismic reflection profiling has been used extensively during the last 25 years in order to unravel crustal structure and evolution, complemented by deep drilling in crystalline rocks. The top and thickness of the highly reflective lower crust as a specific dominant crustal entity correlate with high surface heat flow (Sato *et al.*, 1988). Seismic in-situ velocities are always lower than laboratory-derived or composition-derived velocities. In consequence, crustal composition models inverted from seismic velocity models tend to be biased towards felsic composition. The reason for this is most likely the porosity of crystalline rocks including some hydrothermal activity which may also explain the occurrence of low-velocity zones often observed in the middle crust. Modelling of crustal temperatures, heat transfer and heat production should account for these phenomena.

The relationship between P_n velocity (P wave Velocity at uppermost mantle) has been suggested in various continents of the world including Indian shield (Sharma *et al.*, 1991). They also suggested the correlation among the P_n velocity and Moho temperature, Curie Depth, lithosphere thickness.

Cross-property relations are obtained between the electrical conductivity and seismic velocity using different combinations of the electromagnetic and elastic models (Ursin and Carcione, 2007). The trend is that as the velocity in the overburden (shale saturated with high conductivity brine) increases, the conductivity decreases. The opposite behavior is obtained for the sandstone (saturated with high-resistivity oil).

The attenuation of seismic waves as they travel through the earth is a complex subject. In general, the amplitude of a seismic wave dies off in proportion to the factor e^{-ax}, where x is the distance travelled and 'a' is the attenuation coefficient. The attenuation coefficient is a function of frequency, and it becomes larger as the frequency increases. This preferential attenuation of higher frequencies is a fundamental limitation in seismology that restricts the ability to resolve deep structures because the short wavelengths associated with high frequencies are needed. It is to be noted that 'a' is an approximately linear function of frequency for typical seismic waves. This relationship leads to the quality factor, Q, being a constant. The quality factor is thus a convenient measure of the degree to which a material absorbs seismic energy; high values of Q mean that attenuation is low. An early large-scale observation was that the cold down-going slabs in subduction zones had high Q values while the hot volcanic arcs above the subduction zones had low Q values.

5.6 Applications

The effect of both pressure and temperature on seismic wave velocities must be understood in order to properly interpret the seismologically observed structure of the earth. Similar factors must be considered when sound velocities are compared to the seismically determined radial structure of the earth in order to constrain compositional models (Duffy and Ahrens, 1992).

Seismic techniques provide the highest-resolution measurements of the structure of the crust and have been conducted on a worldwide basis. The structure of the continental crust has been obtained based on the results of seismic refraction profiles and infer crustal composition as a function of depth by comparing these results with high-pressure laboratory measurements of seismic velocity for a wide range of rocks that are commonly found in the crust (Hall and Simmons, 1979; Kaila *et al.*, 1979; Lin and Wang, 1980; Kaila and Krishna, 1992; Christensen and Mooney, 1995; Rao and Tewari, 2008).

P and *S* waves travel at different speed can be used to locate earthquakes. The simple rule of thumb for earthquakes in this distance range is the distance is about eight times the arrival time of S-wave less the arrival time of the P-wave. By studying the propagation characteristics (travel times, reflection amplitudes, dispersion characteristics, etc. of seismic wave detailed nature of earth's interior, the core, the mantle and the crust have been studied for the last 90 years.

Hall and Simmons (1979) measured P- and S-wave velocities on a set of rocks from the Archaean Lewisian metamorphic complex, north-west Britain in the laboratory at confining pressures to 8 kbar. From estimates of velocities at crustal pressures and temperatures, they concluded that the composition of the three crustal layers below the Scottish

Caledonides are most likely to be, in order of increasing depth: (1) mixed metamorphic rocks in amphibolite or lower facies, plus granites, (2) mixed pyroxene-granulite facies rocks, of overall intermediate composition and (3) mafic garnet granulites. Poisson's ratios of isotropic aggregates of mafic amphibolites and serpentinized peridotites in the Lewisian are high (0.28–0.31) because of the presence of hydrous minerals.

Velocities of compressional waves are determined for central California rocks at pressures up to 0.7 GPa (7 kb) and temperatures up to 450°C. These data are used to interpret the seismic velocity structure of the crust in the California Coast Ranges (Lin, and Wang, 1980).

Interval transit time data derived from seismic velocities have been analyzed to predict clay mineralogy and overpressures from compaction trends in the Off shore areas of Krishna-Godavari basin located on the east coast of India. Compaction trends from rms velocity fairly well match the trends obtained from sonic logs. Prospective areas are identified on the basis of clay mineral distribution and overpressure zones related to the areas of different clay mineral associations (Basu, 1990).

Using the P_n velocity and Heat flow relationship for Indian shield (Sharma *et al.*, 1991), the heat flow in some of the parts of the Indian continent where only seismic velocity data is available, has been estimated and geo-thermal structure has been suggested (Sharma *et al.*, 2005, Mall and Sharma, 2009).

In order to interpret the seismic measurements of crustal P-and S-wave velocities, in terms of the experimental results, it is necessary that the geothermal gradient in the area is known (Kern, 1982). Using the following equation,

$$Vp(P, T) = Vp_0 + (dVp/dP)_T.P + (dVp/dT)_p.T \qquad \dots (5.13)$$

Kern and Richter (1981) calculated velocity depth profiles in a cold Precambrian shield crust and in a warm continental crust., based on geotherms reported by Theilen and Meissner (1979).

Christensen and Mooney (1995) summarised the structure of the continental crust based on the results of seismic refraction profiles and infer crustal composition as a function of depth by comparing these results with high-pressure laboratory measurements of seismic velocity for a wide range of rocks that are commonly found in the crust. The thickness and velocity structure of the crust are well correlated with tectonic province, with extended crust showing an average thickness of 30.5 km and orogens an average of 46.3 km. Shields and platforms have an average crustal thickness nearly equal to the global average. The average compressional wave velocity of the crust is 6.45 km/s, and the average velocity of the uppermost mantle (Pn velocity) is 8.09 km/s.

Velocities in the upper continental crust are matched by velocities of a large number of lithologies, including many low-grade metamorphic rocks and relatively silicic gneisses of amphibolite facies grade. In mid-crustal regions, velocity gradients appear to originate from an increase in metamorphic grade, as well as a decrease in silica content. Tonalitic gneiss, granitic gneiss, and amphibolite are abundant midcrustal lithologies. Anisotropy due to preferred mineral orientation is likely to be significant in upper and midcrustal regions. The bulk of the lower continental crust is chemically equivalent to gabbro, with velocities in agreement with laboratory measurements of mafic granulite. Garnet becomes increasingly abundant with depth, and mafic garnet granulite is the dominant rock type immediately above the Mohorovicic discontinuity. Average compressional wave velocities of common crustal rock types show excellent correlations with density (Christensen and Mooney 1995).

5.7 Structure Beneath Deccan Trap Region

Kaila and Krishna (1992) and Rao and Tewari (2008) have reviewed the Deep Seismic Sounding studies in India since 1972. Different profiles across the whole Indian Land mass suggested the crustal structure and Moho depths at corresponding places. Besides mapping the thickness of Deccan trap flows, a large Mesozoic basin, consisting of two grabens separated by an *E-W* trending fault, the 'Tapti graben' (with maximum sedimentary thickness of 1800 m) and 'Narmada graben' (with maximum thickness of 1000 m), is delineated under a relatively thin cover of Deccan Traps in the Narmada-Tapti area from the results obtained along six DSS profiles in the region. The Deccan Traps at the base of thick tertiary sediments, as well as subtrappean Mesozoic sediments in the cambay basin are also well resolved by the DSS datasets. The high velocity lower crustal layer of velocity 7.3–7.4 km/s through out the cambay basin indicates underplating of the crust due to upwelling and rifting with large scale extrusion of Deccan Traps. The region from Surat to Bombay on the west coast was also charaterised by an upwarp of the Moho during the late Cretaceous period, probably representing a transitional crust and major source of Deccan trap flows.

High quality data of seismic velocities can be used to predict underground rock stresses and pore pressure, etc. These velocities are obtained using seismic tomography, which is like a medical X-ray. Seismic reflection tomography allows making maps of the earth's interior to visualize the velocity field. Using seismic tomography, Iyer *et al.* (1989) suggested that few percent higher P wave velocities beneath Deccan Volcanic province in west central India than the surrounding region. This anomaly points to the existence of a large, deep anomalous region in the upper mantle.

CHAPTER VI

Magnetic Properties of Rocks

6.1 Introduction

Magnetism is a phenomenon by which a material exerts either attractive or repulsive force on another. Earth is a giant magnet. Like other magnets, earth has two magnetic poles, north and south, and a magnetic field that attracts charged or "magnetic" objects. The magnetic field has not always been in its present configuration. At times in the past, the poles have reversed or changed direction so that the north magnetic pole becomes south and vice versa. Past reversals of the magnetic field are recorded in the rocks. The remanent magnetization depends on the presence of magnetic minerals. As magma or lava cools, these minerals begin to form. At this point the molten rock has not completely solidified, so the magnetic minerals floating in the molten mass become aligned to the magnetic field. When the rock finally solidifies, these minerals "lock in" the magnetic field as so many tiny compasses. The regional climatic changes during the last glacial maximum are also recorded in the rocks (Liu *et al.*, 2003). Rock magnetism is the study of the magnetic properties of rocks. It includes the study of magnetic minerals. Associated with palaeomagnetism, the purpose of rock magnetism is to understand how magnetic properties of rocks affect the palaeomagnetic data recorded by those rocks. Rock magnetism is one of the oldest sciences known to man. Historians still debate when the magnetic properties of lodestone (or leading stone, a rare natural magnet) were first discovered.

The study of magnetic properties of rocks is, therefore very important to understand the palaeomagnetic data recorded by the rocks. This remanence is carried by minerals, particularly certain strongly magnetic minerals. An understanding of remanence in rocks, sediments and soils helps palaeomagnetists to develop methods for measuring the ancient magnetic field and correct for effects like sediment compaction and metamorphism (Tarling, 1983). The magnetic properties of a given rock may vary widely within a given rock body or structure, depending on chemical in homogeneities, depositional or crystallization conditions, and what happens to the rock after formation.

6.1.1 *Magnetic Fields*

Magnetic fields, like gravitational fields, cannot be seen or touched. We can feel the pull of the Earth's gravitational field on ourselves and the objects around us, but we do not experience magnetic fields in such a direct way. We know of the existence of magnetic fields by their effect on objects such as magnetized pieces of metal, naturally magnetic rocks such as lodestone, or temporary magnets such as copper coils that carry an electrical current. If we place a magnetized needle on a cork in a bucket of water, it will slowly align itself with the local magnetic field. Turning on the current in a copper wire can make a nearby compass needle jump. Observations like these led to the development of the concept of magnetic fields.

6.2 Types of Magnetism

There are three types of basic magnetism:

1. Dia-magnetism
2. Para-magnetism

3. Ferro-magnetism. Anti-Ferro-magnetism and ferry-magnetism are considered as subclasses of Ferro-magnetism.

So the materials may be classified by their response to externally applied magnetic fields as diamagnetic, paramagnetic, or ferromagnetic. These magnetic responses differ greatly in strength.

6.2.1 *Dia-magnetism*

Applied external field acts on atoms of a material, slightly unbalancing their orbiting electrons, and creates small magnetic dipoles within atoms which oppose the applied field. This action produces a negative magnetic effect known as diamagnetism. It is very weak; exists only in presence of an external field, non-permanent. Materials such as Cu, Ag, Si, Ag and alumina are diamagnetic at room temperature.

6.2.2 *Para-magnetism*

When an external field is applied dipoles line-up with the field, resulting in a positive magnetization. Slightly stronger; when an external field is applied dipoles line-up with the field, resulting in a positive magnetization. However, because the dipoles do not interact, extremely large magnetic fields are required to align all of the dipoles. An increase in temperature decreases the paramagnetic effect. Para-magnetism is produced in many materials like aluminum, calcium, titanium, alloys of copper. In the absence of an external field, the orientations of atomic magnetic moments are random leading to no net magnetization.

6.2.3 *Ferro-magnetism*

Both dia- and para-magnetic materials are considered as non-magnetic because they exhibit magnetization only in presence of an external field. Certain materials possess permanent magnetic moments even in the absence of an external field. This is result of permanent unpaired dipoles formed from unfilled energy levels. These dipoles can easily line-up with the imposed magnetic field due to the exchange interaction or mutual reinforcement of the dipoles. These are the characteristics of ferro-magnetism. Materials with ferro-magnetism are Iron, Cobalt and Nickel, etc. An increase in temperature decreases the Ferro-magnetic effect. Above the Curie temperature (≈580°C), ferro-magnetic materials behave as para-magnetic materials. Ferro Magnets are very strong, dipoles line-up permanently upon application of external field. They have two sub-classes i) Ferri-magnetism and ii) Anti-ferro-magnetism.

6.2.3.1 *Ferri-magnetism*

In a magnetic field, the dipoles of a cation may line up with the field, while dipoles of other cation may not. These ceramics are called ferrites, and the effect is known as ferri-magnetism. Some ceramic materials exhibit net magnetization. Fe_3O_4, $NiFe_2O_4$ (Mn.Mg) Fe_2O_4, $PbFe_{12}O_{19}$, $BaFe_{12}O_{19}$, YIG–yttrium iron garnet $Y_3Fe_5O_{12}$ are the ferri- magnetic materials. Below the Neel temperature, therefore, ferromagnetic materials behave very much like ferromagnetic materials and are paramagnetic above the Neel temperature.

6.2.3.2 *Anti-ferro-magnetism*

In a magnetic field, the dipoles line-up, but in opposite directions, resulting in zero magnetization is known as Anti-ferro-magnetism. Mn, Cr, MnO, NiO, CoO, $MnCl_2$ are the example of Anti-ferro-magnetic materials. Exchange interaction which is responsible for parallel alignment of spins is extremely sensitive to inter-atomic spacing and to the atomic positions. This sensitivity causes anti-parallel alignment of spins. When the strength of anti-parallel spin magnetic moments is equal, no net spin moment exists, and resulting susceptibilities are quite small. One noticeable characteristic of anti-ferro-magnets is they attain maximum susceptibility at a critical temperature called Neel temperature. At temperatures above this, anti-ferro-magnets become para-magnetic.

6.3 Magnetic Properties

The magnetic properties of rocks arise from the magnetic properties of the constituent mineral grains and crystals. Typically, only a small fraction of the rock consists of magnetic minerals. It is this small portion of grains that determines the magnetic properties and magnetization of the rock as a whole, with two results: (1) the magnetic properties of a given rock may vary widely within a given rock body or structure, depending on chemical in homogeneities, depositional or crystallization conditions, and what happens to the rock after formation; and (2) rocks that share the same lithology. Magnetic minerals can be classified as Diamagnetic minerals, paramagnetic minerals, ferromagnetic minerals, ferromagnetic minerals, and Antiferro-magnetic minerals.

The magnetic susceptibility of Diamagnetic minerals, as compared to other Para, Ferro, Ferri and Antiferromagnetic minerals is fairly high which is probably caused by a relatively high content of ferromagnetic impurities. Because the paramagnetic susceptibility is controlled by the content of Fe^{2+}, Fe^{3+} and less important of Mn^{2+} (Petersen and Bleil, 1982).

6.3.1 *Magnetic Permeability*

In electromagnetism, permeability is the measure of the ability of a material to support the formation of a magnetic field within itself. In other words, it is the degree of magnetization that a material obtains in response to an applied magnetic field. Magnetic permeability is typically represented by the Greek letter μ. The term was coined in September, 1885 by Oliver Heaviside. The reciprocal of magnetic permeability is magnetic reluctivity.

In SI units, permeability is measured in the henry per metre (Hm^{-1}), or Newton per ampere squared (NA^{-2}). The permeability constant (μ_0), also known as the magnetic constant or the permeability of free space, is a measure of the amount of resistance encountered when forming a magnetic field in a classical vacuum. The magnetic constant has the exact (defined) value $\mu_0 = 4\pi \times 10^{-7} \approx 1.2566370614 \times 10^{-6}$ Hm^{-1} or NA^{-2}).

The magnetization (M) of a material is expressed in terms of density of net magnetic dipole moments (m) in the material. We define a vector quantity called the magnetization 'M' by,

$$M = \mu_{total}/V \quad \ldots (6.1)$$

Then the total magnetic field B in the material is given by,

$$B = B_0 + \mu_0 M \quad \ldots (6.2)$$

Where (μ_0) is the magnetic permeability of free space, and 'B_0' is the externally applied magnetic field. This is just the magnetic field B, which is measured in webers (volt-seconds) per square-metre ($V{\cdot}s/m^2$), or teslas (T).

When magnetic fields inside of materials are calculated using Ampere's law or the Biot-Savart law, then the (μ_0) in those equations is typically replaced by just 'μ' with the definition,

$$\mu = K_m \mu_0 \quad \ldots (6.3)$$

Where, K_m is called the relative permeability. If the material does not respond to the external magnetic field by producing any magnetization, then $K_m = 1$.

6.3.2 *Magnetic Susceptibility*

In electromagnetism, the magnetic susceptibility (c_m) (latin: *susceptibilis* "receptiveness") is the degree of magnetization of a material in response to an applied magnetic field. It is defined as:

$$M = \chi_m H \quad \ldots (6.4)$$

Where, M is magnetization and H is magnetic field.

A magnetic field (H) is generated by passing current I through a coil of length l and number of turns n, then the magnetic field strength, H (units A/m), is given by,

$$H = nI/l \quad \ldots (6.5)$$

Also $\chi_m = \mu_r - 1$ ... (6.6)

Where μ_r is the relative permeability,

and $\mu_r = \mu/\mu_0$ ... (6.7)

Where 'μ_0' is the magnetic permeability of vacuum.

The dependence of susceptibility depends on magnetic field strength results in the difficulty of giving "representative mean values" for ferri- and ferromagnetic minerals (Schon, 1996).

Table 6.1: Mean Values of Susceptibility for Magnetic Minerals

Mineral	*K(SI)*		*Mean*
	Dortman Range	*Telford et al. Range*	
Magnetite	8.8–25	1.2–19.2	6
Ulvospinel	3.8–25	–	–
Maghemite	10^{-5}–10	–	–
Hematite	10^{-4}–10^{-3}	0.5×10^{-3}–3.5×10^{-2}	6.5×10^{-3}
Pyrrhotite	10^{-1}–10^{-2}	10^{-3}–6	1.5
Ilmenite	–	0.3–3.5	1.8
Chromite	10	3×10^{-3}–1.1×10^{-1}	

The mean value susceptibility of some of the magnetic mineral is shown in Table 6.1 for general orientation (Telford *et al.*, 1990).

6.3.3 *Curie Point*

Curie point is also called Curie temperature. It is defined as the temperature at which certain magnetic materials undergo a sharp change in their magnetic properties. In the case of rocks and minerals, remanent magnetism appears below the Curie point- about 580°C for the common magnetic mineral-magnetite. This temperature is named for the French physicist Pierre Curie, who in 1895 discovered the laws that relate some magnetic properties to change in temperature. The antiferro-magnetic Curie point is called the Néel temperature in honor of the French physicist Louis Néel, who in 1936 successfully explained antiferro-magnetism. Determining this temperature can be crucial because it allows us to know at what temperature the ferromagnetic properties will be lost.

Below the Curie point—for example, 770°C (1418°F) for iron—atoms that behave as tiny magnets spontaneously align themselves in certain magnetic materials. In ferromagnetic materials, such as pure iron, the atomic magnets are oriented within each microscopic region (domain) in the same direction, so that their magnetic fields reinforce each other. In antiferro-magnetic materials, atomic magnets alternate in opposite directions, so that their magnetic fields cancel each other. In ferri-magnetic materials, the spontaneous arrangement is a combination of both patterns, usually involving two different magnetic atoms, so that only partial reinforcement of magnetic fields occurs.

Raising the temperature to the Curie point for any of the materials in these three classes entirely disrupts the various spontaneous arrangements, and only a weak kind of more general magnetic behaviour, called paramagnetism, remains. One of the highest Curie points is 1121°C (2050°F) for cobalt. Temperature increases above the Curie point produce roughly similar patterns of decreasing paramagnetism in all three classes of materials.

When these materials are cooled below their Curie points, magnetic atoms spontaneously realign so that the ferro-magnetism, antiferro-magnetism, or ferrimagnetism revive. Curie temperature varies from around 325 to 680°C in magnetic minerals (Piper, 1987; Hunt *et al.*, 1995) is shown above in Table 6.2. However, Curie point is referred to temperature 550 ± 30°C (Mayhew, 1987; Wasilewski and Mayhew, 1992) at which Fe-Ti oxide mineral lose their ferromagnetic property to define the Curie depth in the earth's interior.

Table 6.2: Curie Point of Some of the Magnetic Minerals of the Lower Crust (Wasilewski and Mayhew, 1986; Mayhew, 1987

Mineral	*Composition*	*Tc °C*	*Magnetic State*
Magnetite	Fe_2O_3	580	Ferrimagnetic
Hematite	$\alpha - Fe_2O_3$	680	Antiferromagnetic
Maghaemite	$\beta - Fe_2O_3$	~600	Ferrimagnetic
Pyrrhotite	F_7S_8	325	Ferrimagnetic
Magnesioferrite	$MgFe_2O_4$	440	Ferrimagnetic
Cobalt ferrite	$Co\ Fe_2O_4$	520	Ferrimagnetic
Copper ferrite	$Cu\ Fe_2O_4$	455	Ferrimagnetic
Trevorite	$Ni\ Fe_2O_4$	585	Ferrimagnetic
Awaruite	Ni_3Fe	620	Ferromagnetic
Greigite	Fe_3S_4	~333	Ferrimagnetic

6.4 Measurement Techniques

6.4.1 *Natural Remanent Magnetization (NRM) and Intensity Measurements*

Natural remanent magnetization (NRM) and intensity by using magnetometer (Tarling, 1983), Magnetic susceptibility is measured using susceptibility meter and susceptibility bridge. Curie point is measured subjecting the specimen to thermal demagnetization at certain temperature intervals up to 650°C. This was with a magnetic measurements thermal demagnetizer which comprises a non inductive furnace and continuous degaussed mu-metal shielding (Turner *et al.*, 1983). A wide variety of magnetometers are available (Collinson, 1983). Most of these are designed for 'standard size specimens (Cyliderical with diameter 2.5 cm and 2.1–2.2 cm high, and cubes of side 2.1–2.5 cm) and most of them have similar sensitivities. The Astatic Magnetometer is one of the earliest instrument (Blackett, 1952) in Palaeomagnetic studies and still an important instrument as it is simple yet capable of handling irregularly shaped samples and can also be used to measure low-field susceptibility.

More common in palaeomagnetic laboratories are Spinner magnetometers in which standard specimens are spun near a pick-up coil (Tarling, 1983). The rotating magnetization induces a current in the pick-up coil, the amplitude of which depends on the intensity of magnetization of the specimen in the perpendicular to the axis of rotation, while its direction within that plane is given by the phase angle. One of the fastest and more sensitive of these types of magnetometer uses airing fluxgate pick-up system and is linked to a micro-computer unit for precise determination of the phase angle and amplitude (Molyneux, 1971; Collinson, 1983). This, and similar instruments, takes from 2 to 20 minutes to measure the direction and the total intensity of the remanence, again depending upon the magnetic moment of the specimen. Adequate measurements can usually be made in some 20 minutes for magnetic moments as low as 5×10^{-10} Am^2 (5×10^{-5} Am^{-1} intensity for standard 2.5×2.1 cm cylinders). Only standard sized samples can be measured in this way. A large specimen version is available (mostly for archaeomagnetic work) for cylinders 5.5 cm in diameter, 5.1 cm high. Modifications of this large access magnetometer can also be used to measure the horizontal component of remanence in long cores of sediment (Tarling, 1983).

Cryogenic Magnetometers are complex systems that basically comprise a ring that is maintained at liquid helium temperatures. These instruments are capable of good sensitivities. Small access cryogenic magnetometers are also available and have higher sensitivities for special studies. The main advantage of such magnetometers over all other magnetometers is not the somewhat greater sensitivity, but the fact that each measurement can be made in only a few seconds (Tarling, 1983). Cryogenic magnetometers and other magnetometers are well described in detail by Collinson (1983).

6.4.2 *Susceptibility Measurement*

A variety of methods exists for measurement of the high–or low field susceptibility of rock specimens (Collinson, 1983). One common type is the bridge (a) in which the specimen unbalanced the circuit according to its susceptibility and electrical conductivity. The imbalance is normally a direct measure of the susceptibility of the specimen inserted within the air gap. The anisotropy of susceptibility is usually measured (b) by a system in which one set of coils produces a magnetic field. If a specimen in this is magnetically isotropic, the no field is detected by the pick-up coils (Collinson and Molyneux,

1967). If the specimen is magnetically anisotropic, then a voltage is induced in the pick-up coils that are dependent on the anisotropy of the specimen. Computer systems can be used to determine the shape of the mean magnetic ellipsoid from three orthogonal rotations of the specimen within the instrument. Although conventionally regarded as the magnetization acquired in fields below 10^{-2} T, most instruments are designed for applied fields of less than 10^{-3} T as this avoids the possible addition of isothermal remanence to the specimen.

6.4.3 *Magneto Anisotropic Measurement*

Any alignment of magnetic mineral shapes or their crystalline axes gives rise to a magnetic anisotropy that may significantly affect the degree of alignment of natural remanence with ambient field within which it was acquired (Tarling, 1983). Two main instruments are available for the determination of the low field magnetic anisotropy of specimens (Collinson, 1983).

6.4.4 *Curie Temperature Measurement*

The heating of a sample will induce chemical changes in its magnetic and also non-magnetic minerals, resulting in the creation and destruction of magnetic minerals at certain temperatures, some of which can be diagnostic of changing mineralogy involved. Some of these changes can also indicate that the sample has never previously been heated to that temperature as observed chemical interaction would have already taken place, but these changes can also occur in fresh igneous rocks, reflecting the radically different environment of laboratory heating when compared with natural conditions, particularly in the redox conditions that cannot be readily be duplicated in the laboratory. By far the simplest method of making such analyses is by means of studies of the saturation magnetization as a function of temperature, i.e. the curves used Curie temperature determinations, as these show increase or decrease in the induced magnetic moment as chemical changes after the magnetic mineralogy (Tarling, 1983). The procedure to determine the Curie temperature by Curie Balance is to heat a specimen of a rock while holding it in a strong magnetic field. The magnetization is measured as the specimen heated. Two main types of Curie balance exist, although several types are available (Collinson, 1983).

6.5 Relationship between Magnetic Properties and Geophysical Parameters

6.5.1 *Magnetic Susceptibility and Density of Rocks*

The density of igneous and metamorphic rocks is very closely related to mineral composition. Many genetic processes generating the mineral composition will be reflected in the density of rocks (Henkel, 1976). For acid plutonic rocks, density is controlled by the amount of mafic minerals, while in basic rocks, the amount of plagioclase is determinative (Henkel, 1976). Other possible factors are nature of mafics present, percentage of opaques or high density accessories.

The magnetic properties are useful indicators of the geochemical and petro- logical state of a rock (Lapointe *et al.*, 1984). The magnetic properties depend essentially on the characteristics of a small group of magnetic carrier minerals that are universal constituents of all rocks. The magnetic minerals generally belong to the ternary system FeO-Fe_2O_3-TiO_2 which include magnetite, titano-magnetite, haematite, ilmenite and rutile. Magnetic minerals have in general high density. The magnetic susceptibility of a rock does not wholly depend on the amount of iron oxides present, but is mainly influenced by the quantity of iron oxides in ferromagnetic minerals. The main ferrimagnetic mineral is magnetite apart from the members of the titano-magnetic series and pyrhotite. Aravamadhu (1974) estimated susceptibilities of charnockite samples from the South Indian shield and observed a linear relationship between the magnetite content and susceptibility values. Density of the rocks also depends on the high density minerals like magnetite. Densities and magnetic susceptibilities of Precambrian rocks from South Indian Shield have been estimated by Subrahmanyam and Verma (1981). Densities and magnetic susceptibilities of metamorphic rocks from South Indian Granulite terrain have been estimated by Ramachandran and Bosu (1991) and Ramachandran (1992) respectively. Ramachandran (1992) estimated petro-physical properties of granulite rocks in the southern Indian shield. Petrophysical properties of some dolerite dykes of Andhra Pradesh have been analyzed by Varaprasada Rao *et al.* (1978).

The Susceptibility is controlled mainly by the content of Fe^{2+}, Fe^{3+}, an empirical correlation between susceptibility, χ_m and Fe content C_{Fe} (in weight %) is recommended for practical applications,

$$\chi_m = 3.48\ C_{Fe} \qquad \ldots (6.8)$$

Where 'χ_m' is in $m^3\ kg^{-1}$. This correlation was derived for the minerals, garnet, tourmaline, biotite, muscovite, amphibole, cordierite, and pyroxene with Fe content between 0 and 30 weight % (Schon, 1996).

6.5.2 *Curie Temperature and Heat Flow*

Curie depth depends upon Curie temperature which varies from350 to 680°C in magnetic minerals (Piper, 1987). However Curie point in the crust is referred to a temperature of 550 + 30°C at which Fe-Ti oxide minerals lose their ferromagnetic property ((Mayhew, 1987; Wasilewski and Mayhew, 1992). A linear correlation between Curie depth and heat flow cannot be expected due to large variation in Curie temperatures of the minerals. It is observed that the Curie depth in non uniform and may range from 6–40 km (Shuey *et al.*, 1977; Lachenbruch and Sass, 1978; Mayhew, 1982, Negi *et al.*, 1987) based upon the data of Mayhew (1982) and Indian data suggested that the heat flow decreases exponentially with an increase in Curie depth. However the relationship between Heat flow (Qs) and Curie depth (H) can be better represented by the function with a correlation factor of 0.99 (Sharma *et al.*, 2005),

$$Qs = 640H^{0.68} \qquad \text{... (6.9)}$$

Cathrine *et al.* (2005) computed heat flow anomalies using Curie depths observed by Satellite Magnetic data.

6.5.3 *Curie Temperature and Electrical Conductivity*

In investigating the electric conductivity of rocks stress σ as a function of the temperature it was found that rocks containing ferri-magnetic minerals display a change in the slope of the function $\sigma = f(1/T)$ in the neighborhood of the Curie temperature (Lagtovikowl and Kropick, 1976; Sharma, 1982). This relation between and the changes in the pattern of the electric conductivity is caused by the variations of the exchangeable energy of ferrimagnetic minerals (Lagtovikowl and Kropick, 1976). The DC electrical conductivity was studied as a function of both composition and temperature for the ferrite system $Ni_xMg_{1-x}Fe_2O_4$ prepared by the usual ceramic technique. The experimental results proved that, the DC electrical conductivity increases as the temperature increases and as the nickel ion content and porosity decrease. The Curie temperature and the activation energies for electrical conduction increase as the nickel ion content increases.

6.5.4 *Curie Depth and Seismic Velocity*

Compressional wave velocity at the uppermost mantle (P_n) may be an indicator of thermal conditions prevailing in the crust (Sharma *et al.*, 1991). Also, Curie depth indicates the temperature of the demagnetization (Curie temperature) of the magnetic minerals present in the lower crust. Using the heat flow data of the Indian shield and estimating the Curie temperature in the crust and the P_n velocity reported beneath the Indian Shield. Sharma *et al.* (1991) suggested a correlation between the P_n velocity and Curie depth (Z_c) as:

$$P_n = 7.08 + 18.7 \times 10^{-3} Z_c \qquad \ldots (6.10)$$

This indicates that the low P_n velocity is associated with shallow Curie depth. Similar results have also been reported by Cull and Denham (1979), Black and Brail (1982), Kubik (1986, 1988).

6.6 Applications

Most archaeological materials and rocks contain magnetic particles, if only as impurities, they will have magnetic properties that can be used in a variety of ways (Tarling, 1983). One of the main properties is that they may acquire a remanence at some specific time. Magnetic property investigation is essentially useful on such rock types which range from ultramafic to felsic and found in plutonic, hypabyssal and volcanic association that throw light on their evolutionary history. Identification of the magnetic carrier and inference of its domain state are very important in any palaeomagnetic study (Rao *et al.*, 2000) in order to rely on the remanent magnetic signature isolated from it. As the geomagnetic field changes direction and intensity in both time and space, the time of this acquisition can be determined by comparison of these magnetic parameters with known records of the past geomagnetic field at that locality.

Magnetic properties provide cheap, effective, non-destructive techniques that have an application in a wide variety of Archaeological problems.

6.6.1 *Archaeomagnetic Dating*

Magnetic observatory records indicate that the earth's magnetic field gradually changes in direction and intensity by amounts that differ from one part of the globe to another and also differ in time at the same locality. Archaeomagnetic dating can be undertaken with unoriented samples, using intensity, or with oriented samples, using both the intensity and direction of remanence. The actual magnetic properties can also be used in a variety of ways. The rate at which a sample acquires a viscous magnetization can be used as another way of archaeomagnetic dating (Tarling, 1983).

6.6.2 *Other Archaeological Applications*

Archaeomagnetic dating has been undertaken for many years. Even fewer are the considerations of how the magnetization of archaeological materials can be utilized in other ways. The main application of this property has been in terms of geophysical exploration using portable magnetometers to detect the presence of materials with a different susceptibility or remanence compared with the surroundings (Aitken, 1974, Tarling, 1983). There are few studies of the ways in which magnetic properties of archaeological material can be utilized. The iron impurity content of the cast metals may, for example, reflect the technological state of smelting, as well as the types of ore being used and hence provenance. Like wise study of old coins, composition of the die, study of old statue, thermal demagnetization of different stages (Tarling, 1983.) can have applications to use the magnetic properties.

6.6.3 *Geomagnetic Applications*

The geomagnetic field is one of the most intriguing aspects of the earth and is also one of the earliest geophysical properties to be studied scientifically (Gilbert, 1600) yet its origin can still be loosely explained in terms of magneto-hydrodynamic motions in the earth's outer core. An understanding of the origin and behavior of the geomagnetic field is therefore crucial to any understanding of the core itself, interaction between the core and mantle, and the origin of the earth itself. Conversely, much of the information on the properties of the core and lower mantle is based on geomagnetic observations (Tarling, 1983). Information on the strength and direction of the geomagnetic field comes from three main sources-magnetic observatories, surveys on land and sea, and satellite measurements. Observatory and survey records show that the geomagnetic field undergoes long term changes, secular variations on time scale longer than one year (excluding the 11 year sun-spot cycle, and these variations differ in magnitude from one observatory to another, although there has been an average tendency for the total magnetic field strength to decrease (Peterson, 1974). It is generally considered that the non-dipole field arises from convective disturbances near the core-mantle boundary and, until recently, that the westward drift of the field arises from the difference in rotation rates between the earth's core and mantle. Any fuller understanding requires a much closure definition of the nature of secular variations and polarity changes over much longer time scales than are available from observatory records. The available palaeomagnetic data already provide major constraints on many postulated mechanisms, although considerably more observations, with much higher precision, are still required (Tarling, 1983). A major contribution from archaeomagnetic studies is the clear evidence that both eastward and westward drift of the magnetic field have occurred during archaeological time (Kovacheva, 1982).

Present day lake sediments provide an invaluable, nearly continuous record of geomagnetic changes at one particular location, usually for periods of 10–15000 years, and mostly since the end of the last Ice Age (Verosub and Banerjee, 1977). Some lake sediments can be extremely accurately dated. It is possible to count the varves back from the present day, thus establishing a chronology that is accurate, in absolute terms, to within absolute limits of 300–475 years even 10,000 years ago. Even where such an absolute scale does not exist, it is possible to undertake varve counts within an exposed section and determine the duration of the sedimentation record even though its absolute age is unknown (Verosub, 1979).

Although dating method are generally too imprecise for determination of the periodicity and sense of motion of the secular variations of the geomagnetic field for materials older than some 100,000 or so years, palaeomagnetic observations can still be used to assess the magnitude of such variations and therefore to test models of their origin (Tarling, 1983).

6.6.4 *Polarity Reversals*

The evidence for terrestrial polarity changes is based on palaeomagnetic observations alone and it is obviously critical to establish that the observed polarity changes are attributed to geomagnetic changes and not to some physical, self reversal mechanism occurring in the certain rocks (Tarling, 1983). The polarity change in geomagnetic field is, in fact, overwhelming. The same polarity change can be dated at exactly the same time in both sediments and igneous rocks. For the last 150 million years or so, the most detailed record of geomagnetic polarity changes provided by the analyses of magnetic anomaly patterns observed in the ocean basin. The oceanic crust acts as a tape-recorder of the polarity changes of geomagnetic field (Tarling, 1983). Irving and Pulliah (1976) have attempted to assess the average polarity of geomagnetic field during the last 600 Ma by comparison of the number of sites reported to have normal polarity and those with reversal polarity.

6.6.5 *Magnetic Dating*

The occurrence of magnetic minerals in virtually all rocks means that palaeomagnetic studies can be applied in a very wide range of context. In particular, rocks can be magnetically dated on a range of scales, from 1 to 10^8 years. Magnetic dating can be undertaken over a range of time scales using the intensity and direction of remanence, and also its various components. The geological interpretations that have been made on the basis of palaeomagnetic data appear to provide sensible interpretations that are consistent with other geological data indicates that such geomagnetic models are valid (Tarling, 1983).

6.6.6 *Sedimentological Applications*

Many types of sediment were characterized by directions that did not always correspond to the geomagnetic field at the time of their deposition. It is possible to investigate magnetically the processes that have caused such deviations in sediments. The variation of magnetic minerals within soil can itself be of value in deciphering their history (Mullins, 1977). It can be expected that the composition and concentration of magnetic mineral in successive years still tend to influence in response to change in the hydrological regime that are predominantly controlled by climate variability. Variations in the intensity of remanence and in susceptibility will also tend to reflect climatic changes. It is unlikely that the composition of the magnetic mineral being deposited in deep oceanic sediments was changed significantly, except by major meteoric showers or extensive volcanic eruptions, and so most observed changes are more likely to reflect changes in the rate of deposition of non-detrital materials, such as carbonates (Tarling, 1983). Combined sedimentological and palaeomagnetic studies provide an elegant and potentially precise way of differentiating which processes have been of the most importance in indifferent sediments and also offer the potential possibility of their magnetic dating (Alagarsamy, 2009).

6.6.7 *Structural Applications*

There has been a tremendous expansion in the use of palaeomagnetic methods to detect and measure the relative rotation of different tectonic units on both a global and subcontinental scale. In virtually all cases the data requirements are similar. The individual samples must be stably magnetized and the stable component must reflect the direction of the local geomagnetic field at known time. Structure applications of palaeomagnetism deals the problems that can and have been tackled palaemagnetically—problems related to Inter-continental movements (Norton and Sclater, 1979).

6.6.8 *Biological, Weather, Climate, Palaeontological and Palaeo-Geographic Aspects*

There is increasing evidence for subtle influences of geomagnetic changes on animal and plant behavior (Tarling, 1983). There are strong connections between climatic zones and the distribution of different life forms on the present earth, and such relationships can be shown to have existed in the past (Turner and Tarling 1982). There are also some indications that changes in geomagnetic properties can also have direct effects on both life forms (Knox *et al.*, 1979) and the weather (Wollin *et al.*, 1971). The main contribution of palaeomagnetic studies is likely to assess the past palaeo-latitudes and palaeo-geographies and determining, in particular, the distribution of life forms under such conditions. Such evolutions are particularly important in palaeontological evaluation as the classification of fossils (Tarling, 1983).

6.6.9 *Extraterrestrial Studies*

The study of the magnetic field of the other planets is fundamental to any understanding of their origin, and important in evaluating the possible processes operating within the earth which are causing the observed magnetic behavior. Most of the information has been obtained by satellite probes carrying magnetometers, although studies on meteorites and lunar samples can be carried out directly (Tarling, 1983). Such direct studies are particularly critical as they indicate the nature of past magnetic fields and are thus essential to any studies on the interactions with the solar wind and hence atmospheric and climatic evolutionary processes on other planets (Cordell, 1980) as well as on the earth. Studies on lunar samples, in particular, have demonstrated the existence of a previous intrinsic magnetic field that no longer exists on the moon (Daily and Dyal, 1979).

6.6.10 *Lower Crustal Composition*

Magnetic properties of the crust using aeromagnetic and satellite measurements above the surface are studied to understand the nature of the magnetic source at depth. Surface heat flow provides the information regarding the subsurface temperature distribution in the crust (Gupta *et al.*, 1991), which affects magnetic properties (Shive *et al.*, 1992). Laboratory measurements of magnetic properties of crustal/mantle rocks provide the magnetic characteristics. Magnetic anomalies are produced in the crust by rock bodies that contain 5% or more magnetite by volume and located above 600°C isotherms in the crust (Shive *et al.*, 1992). However, lower crustal rocks, which are basic and ultramafic in nature, may contain other magnetic minerals apart from magnetite (Kletetschka and Stout, 1998). Majority of the studies on magnetic properties of the lower crustal show that the magnetite (Fe_3O_4) with at most a few percent of Ulvospinel (Fe_2TiO_4) in solid solution is the dominant magnetic mineral in the lower crust (Shive *et al.*, 1992). However, other magnetic minerals could also be the possible source of deep crustal and upper mantle magnetization (Toft and Haggerty, 1988).

Curie depth depends upon Curie temperature, which varies from around 325 to 680°C in magnetic minerals in the deep crust/upper mantle (Piper, 1987). However, Curie point is referred to temperature 550 + 30°C (Mayhew, 1982) at which Fe-Ti oxide minerals lose their magnetic property. The Curie temperature of magnetite increases at the rate of 1.85°C/k bar (Schult, 1970) and remanent and induced magnetization may be similarly affected by pressure. So it is reasonably good to consider that rocks should lose their magnetization at a depth corresponding to 600°C isotherm (Shive *et al.*, 1992). Sharma *et al.* (2006) explained that the mismatch between the Curie depths estimated using Magnetic Satellite data and heat flow data could be due to the variation in magnetic mineral composition in the lower crust.

6.6.11 *Hydrocarbon Exploration*

Hydrocarbon deposits are generally formed under suitable climate, organic carbon burial and physic-chemical conditions, controlled by overall basin tectonics (Irving *et al.*, 1974). Continental reconstruction, based on palaeomagnetic observations, show that many such hydrocarbon deposits occur within 35° of the palaeo-equator during most of the Phanerozoic period (last 600 Ma) (Irving *et al.*, 1974). However, there are some exceptions to this fact (Rao and Rao, 2007). Palaeo-magnetic study of a number of meso-Neo Proterozoic Vindhyan Super group formations in India over the last one decade, resulted in palaeo-latitudes of 35–40° of the palaeo-equator that are favourable for transformation and preservation of oil resources (Rao and Rao, 2007).

6.7 Studies in Deccan Traps

6.7.1 *Magnetic Properties of Deccan Basalts and their Correlations with Other Physical Properties*

Magnetic susceptibility and magnetic intensity on Deccan basalts from Latur, area of Deccan Trap Region where deep crustal earthquakes occurred in the past, have been measured at NTP conditions. Sample of Deccan basalts were collected from two different flows of Latur area. Density and porosity on the same samples have also been measured to understand the correlation among magnetic and these physical properties (Sharma *et al.*, 2004). The results show that magnetic susceptibility of Latur basalts varies from 9 to 24.5 × 10^{-3} SI units and the intensity varies from 0.4 to 6.39 A/m which indicates the variation in crystallization temperature and environmental conditions of the solidification (Sharma *et al.*, 2004). The relationship between Magnetic susceptibility and Magnetic Intensity, Magnetic intensity and density, and magnetic susceptibility and density of Deccan basalts from two different flows of Latur area are shown in Figures 6.1, 6.2 and 6.3 respectively.

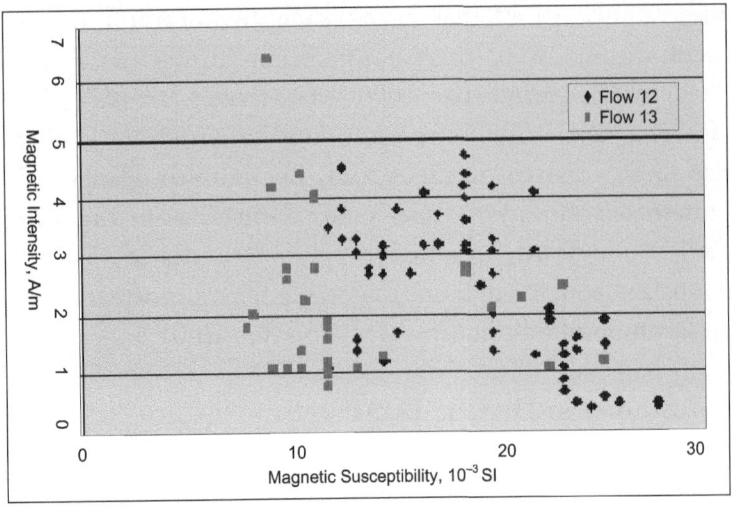

Fig. 6.1: Relationship between Magnetic Susceptibility and Intensity in Basalts from Latur Area, Deccan Traps

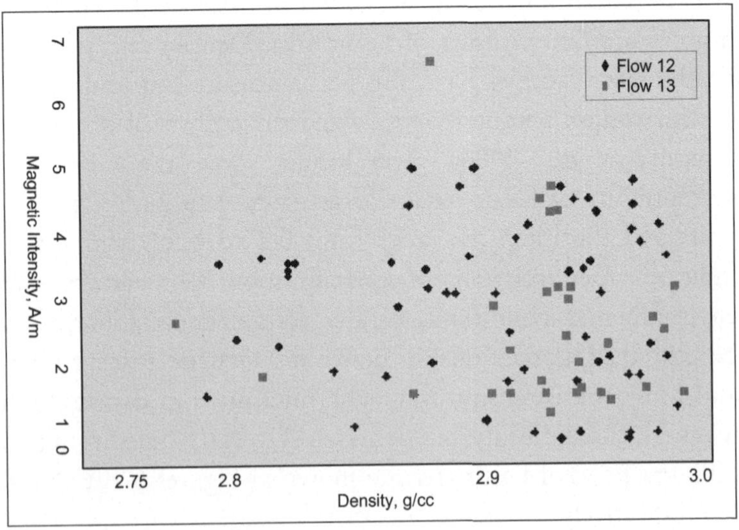

Fig. 6.2: Relationship between Magnetic Intensity and Density in Basalts from Latur Area, Deccan Traps

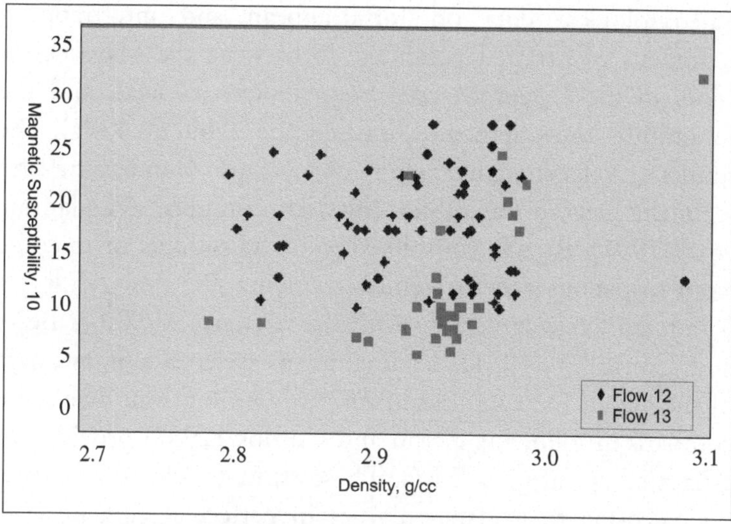

Fig. 6.3: Relationship between Magnetic Susceptibility and Density in Basalts from Latur Area, Deccan Traps

These figures indicate that the samples which show high density and high magnetic susceptibility most likely consist of more ferromagnetic magnetic minerals as compared to other samples. This could be correlated to the source of magma and crystallization conditions. The magnetic susceptibility and magnetic intensity does not have any 1:1 correlation, but above conclusion can also be drawn from this relationship (Sharma *et al.* (2004).

6.7.2 *Palaeomagnetic Measurements*

Detailed palaeomagnetic measurements have been made on a lava sequence exposed between altitudes of 700 to 1000 meters in the Amarkantak-Dindori tract on the eastern margin of the Deccan traps (Athavale, 1970). These data are at variance with the observation of the same reversal of magnetic field at an altitude of about 625 meters in the palaeomagnetic study of several other vertical sequences in the Deccan traps.

Paleontological data on infratrappean and intertrappean sediments constrain Deccan age to between the Mayaroensis zone, in the Upper Maestrichtian (about 67 Ma), and the foraminifer zone, in the Lower Paleocene (about 60.5 Ma). The results of Palaeomagnetic study of a Nagpur-Bombay traverse from the Deccan traps (563 flows) are compiled (Vandamme *et al.*, 1991). Results considered to be transitional or to come from suspicious sites are removed leaving 485 flow results. It is in remarkable agreement with the reference APWP of Besse and Courtillot (1991), leading to an independent estimate of the age of Deccan volcanism at 67.2 ± 6.6 Ma. The same comparison following Acton and Gordon (1989) provides an estimated age at 67 ± 5 Ma. These estimates which are based on paleo-magnetic data only are in perfect agreement with both radiometric and paleontological ages.

A compilation of 35 magnetic studies (Vandamme and Courtillot, 1992) confirms the general applicability of the Normal-Reversed-Normal (NRN) model and reveals the large-scale topography of the RN boundary, which is an isochron, over most of the Deccan. The RN isochron surface displays a boomerang shape, with topography ranging from sea-level to above 1600 m. This observed topography is consistent with a simple model in which doming and renewed rifting and dyke intrusion resulted from Impingement, 70–65 Ma ago, of the Reunion plume under the Indian lithosphere. The Narmada-Son rift was rejuvenated and a continental rift system with minor extension with a triple junction in the Cambay Graben resulted and was subsequently covered by the Deccan flows, although in places tectonic faulting and volcanism continued to interfere. The Rajahmundry outcrops constrain the original extended southeastward dip away from the triple junction of much of the traps, a significant part of which has now been removed by erosion and rifting away of the Seychelles.

6.7.3 *Palaeomagnetic Study in Lonar Crater*

Lonar crater in India is one of the youngest and best preserved impact structures on earth. The 1.88 km diameter simple crater formed entirely within the Deccan traps, making it a useful analogue for small craters on the basaltic surfaces of the other terrestrial planets and the moon. The palaeomagnetic and rock-magnetic properties of this crater have been investigated in order to understand the effect of impacts on magnetization in target rocks (Louzada *et al.*, 2008). The magnetization in the Lonar basalts consists of an original 65 Ma Deccan magnetization and a recent over print. They also did not find the evidence of shock demagnetization or the presence of intense impact-induced or impact amplified transient magnetic fields that have been proposed around larger impact structures. However, based on the Palaeomagnetic and rock magnetic investigations carried out on oriented rock samples collected from the inner walls of Lonar Lake, Rao and Bhalla (1984) has shown palaeomagnetic evidence of shock origin of Lonar Lake.

CHAPTER VII

Natural Radioactivity in Rocks and Minerals

7.1 Introduction

Natural radioactivity is the spontaneous transformation of an unstable atom (natural radio nuclides) of certain isotopes into other isotopes and often results in the emission of radiations. This process is referred to as a transformation, decay or a disintegration of an atom. The decay process is described by its probability. A given nuclide has a probability of decay per unit time which is independent of any external condition if the resultant isotope is not stable, it will undergo further decay until finally a stable isotope is formed. The decay process, usually accompanied by emission of alpha, beta, and gamma radiations. Natural gamma ray radiation is one form of spontaneous radiations emitted by unstable nuclei. Gamma (γ) radiation may be considered either as an electromagnetic wave similar to visible light or X-rays, or as a particle of photon. Gamma rays are electromagnetic radiations emitted from an atomic nucleus during radioactive decay, with the wavelength in the range of 10^{-9} to 10^{-11} cm.

Radioactive Material is any material that contains radioactive atoms. Radioactive elements are often called radioactive isotopes or radio-nuclides or just nuclides. There are over 1,500 different radioactive nuclides. Radio-nuclides are found naturally in air, water and soil. They are even found in us, being that we are products of our environment. Every day, we ingest and inhale radio-nuclides in our air and food and the water. Natural radioactivity is common in the rocks and soil that makes up our planet, in water and oceans, and in our building materials and homes. There is nowhere on earth that you cannot find Natural Radioactivity. Isotopes naturally found on earth are usually those which are stable or which have a decay time larger than, or at least a significant fraction of the age of the earth (about 5×10^9 years). Isotopes with shorter half life mainly exist as decay products from longer lived isotopes, and, as in C^{14}, from irradiation of the upper atmosphere. Radioisotopes with a sufficiently long half life and whose decay produces an appreciable amount of gamma rays are:

- Potassium ^{40}K with half life of 1.3×10^9 years, which emits 0 α, 1 β, and 1 γ-ray.
- Thorium ^{232}Th with half life of 1.4×10^{10} years, which emits 7 α, 5 β, and numerous γ-ray with different energies.
- Uranium ^{238}U with half-life of 4.4×10^9 years, which emits 8 α, 6 β, and numerous γ-ray with different energies.

Each of these elements emits gamma-rays with distinctive energy.

The natural radioactivity of rocks is due to the decay of natural radionuclide found in the rocks and minerals. Radioactive heat production is a scalar and isotropic petro-physical property independent of in situ temperature and pressure. All natural radioactive isotopes generate heat to a certain extent but only the contribution of the decay series of Uranium, Thorium and Potassium is significant. These elements are singled out for special attention because their radioactivity gives the unique importance to the thermal budget of the earth and the terrestrial planets. The concentrations of these elements can be converted to rates of heat production (Birch, 1954). Heat production due to the presence of these elements in the earth's crust and mantle is one of the motive forces behind all geodynamic processes.

It is an important parameter which plays a dominant role in interpreting terrestrial heat flow patterns and in calculating thermal models. The partial disintegration (spontaneous decay) of the nuclei of radioactive elements provides decay particles and energy. The energy, composed of emission kinetic energy and radiation, is converted to heat; it has been an important factor in affecting the temperature gradient and thermal evolution of the earth. Deep-seated elevated temperatures provide the heat that causes rock to deform plastically and to move, thus generating to a large extent the processes of plate tectonics-plate motions, sea floor spreading, continental drift, and subduction and most earthquakes and volcanism.

7.2 Units of Radioactivity

7.2.1 *Becquerel (Bq)*

The Becquerel is a unit used to measure a radioactivity. One Becquerel is the quantity of a radioactive material that will have 1 transformation in one second. Often radioactivity is expressed in larger units like: thousands (KBq), one millions (MBq) or even billions (GBq) of a Becquerel. As a result of having one Becquerel being equal to one transformation per second, there are 3.7×10^{10} Bq in one curie. Many of the units used in science are broken down into smaller units or expressed as multiples, using standard metric prefixes.

7.2.2 *Curie (Ci)*

The curie is a unit used to measure a radioactivity. One curie is that quantity of a radioactive material that will have 3.7×10^{10} transformations in one second. Often radioactivity is expressed in smaller units like thousandths (mCi), one millionths (μCi) or even billionths (nCi) of a curie. The relationship between Becquerel and Curie is 3.7×10^{10} Bq in one Curie.

7.3 Radioactivity in Minerals and Rocks

It is caused by the naturally occurring radioactive elements in the mineral's composition. The degree of radioactivity is dependent on the concentration and isotope present in the mineral. For the most part, minerals that contain potassium (K), uranium (U), and thorium (Th) are radioactive. The heat generated within rocks depends on the types and abundances of the radioactive elements and their host minerals. Such heat production, *A,* is given in calories per cubic centimeter per second, or 1 calorie per gram per year = 4.186×10^7 ergs per gram per year = 1.327 ergs per gram per second. The rate of radioactive decay, statistically an exponential process, is given by the half-life ($t_{1/2}$). The half-life is the time required for half the original radioactive atoms to decay for a particular isotope. The isotopic abundance is the percent of the natural element that exists as that particular radioactive isotope. Mineral radioactivity is due to alpha (α), beta (β) and gamma (γ) radiations from the unstable isotopes in the composition. Radioactive elements, their abundance, half life and types of decay radiation are shown in Table 7.1.

Table 7.1: Radioactive Elements, their Abundance, Half Life and Types of Decay Radiation

Element	*Isotope Symbol*	*Natural Abundance*	*Half-life (Years)*
Thorium	^{232}Th	100.00%	1.4×10^{10}
Uranium	^{238}U	99.28%	4.46×10^9
Potassium	^{40}K	0.01%	1.25×10^9
Uranium	^{235}U	0.72%	0.704×10^9

The radioactive elements are more concentrated in the continental upper-crust rocks that are rich in quartz (*i.e.,* acidic, or less mafic). This results because these rocks are differentiated by partial melting of the upper-mantle and oceanic-crust rock. The radioactive elements tend to be preferentially driven off from these rocks for geochemical reasons. The heat depends on the amounts of uranium, thorium and potassium present in rock. So it varies with rock type over several orders of magnitude and reflects the geochemical conditions. For the rocks, the typical content is given for uranium and thorium (in parts per million [ppm] of weight) and for potassium (in weight percent). The heat production of natural uranium is close to that for the isotope U-238, since almost all natural uranium is of that isotopic species. A compilation of heat productivities of various rock types (Schon, 1996) is given in Table 7.2.

Table 7.2: Mean Uranium, Thorium and K Content of Igneous Rocks

Rock Type	*U ppm*	*Th ppm*	*K%*	*Th/U*
Granite	4 –7	15–40	3.4–40	3.5–5.6
Granodiorite	2.1	8.3	2.3	4.0
Diorite	1.8	6.0	1.8	3.3
Gabbro, Diabase	0.6	1.8	0.7	3.0
Dunite, Pyroxene	0.03	0.08	0.15	2.7
Basalts	0.7	2.3	1.0	3.2

Contents and content ratios (Th/U, K/U and K/Th) show a distinct dependence and correlation to genetic conditions (Haack, 1982):

- Granites and granodiorites above subduction zones have lower U, Th and K concentrations than granites which are not above subduction zones.
- Volcanics show various contents and ratios for different geotectonic positions. Lava shows different contents and ratios depending on chemical and mineralogical composition (Schon, 1996).

The granites show relatively high U-contents and a distinct difference between the granite types (Simov, 1989; Gupta *et al.*, 1991).

7.3.1 *Calculation of Radioactive Heat Production in Rocks*

Radioactive heat production (A) is a scalar and isotropic petro-physical property independent of in situ temperature and pressure. Its value is usually expressed in HGU units (1 HGU = 10^{-13} cal/cm^3 sec) and depends on the amounts of uranium, thorium and potassium. 'A' varies with rock type over several orders of magnitude and reflects the geochemical conditions during rock formation (magmatic differentiation, sedimentation or metamorphism), preferentially driven off from these rocks for geochemical reasons. The heat production of a given radioactive isotope depends upon its radiation energy and half life. The heat production constants of Birch (1954) which give the heat generated per unit time and gram U, Th and K are generally accepted and extensively used in the literature. Since 1954, however, decay schemes, half lives and mass differences have been revised (Hyde *et al.*, 1964). This calls for the redetermination of the heat production constants.

During radioactive decay mass is converted to energy. This energy is set free as the kinetic energy of the involved particles and nuclei (α and β-particles, recoil nuclei) and as the energy of the accompanying (γ) radiation. Except the amount carried away by the neutrino the whole decay energy is converted to heat (Hurley and Fairbairn, 1953). The revised heat production constants for natural uranium (99.28% U^{238}, 0.711% U^{235}), U^{238}, U^{235}, thorium and potassium (with 0.0118% K^{40}) are given in Table 7.3.

Radioactive heat production in a given rock can be calculated, using the constants of Table 7.3, if its uranium, thorium and potassium contents (C_u, C_{Th} and C_K) are known. Practical concentration units are weight ppm for uranium and thorium and weight percent for potassium.

Table 7.3: Revised Heat Production Constants

Element Decay Series	*A [cal/g, y]*	
	Rybach (1976)	*Birch (1954)*
^{238}U	0.692	0.71
^{235}U	4.34	4.3
U (natural)	0.718	0.73
Th^{232}	0.193	0.20
K (natural)	$26.2.10^{-6}$	27.10^{-6}

Heat production is usually given in HGU units

(1 HGU = 10^{-13}cal/cm^3, sec), taking the density ρ(g/cm^3) into account:

$$A \{HGU\} = 0.317\rho\ (0.718\ C_u + 0.193C_{Th} + 0.262C_K) \quad \ldots (7.1)$$

7.4 Experimental Determination of Heat Production

In common rocks uranium and thorium are present in trace amounts only. Numerous analytical techniques exist which enable the determination of these low concentrations (1 ppm = 10^{-6}g/g): Fluorimetry, activation analysis, delayed neutrons, fission track counting, mass spectrometry. Potassium can be determined by flame photometry, atomic absorption, X-ray fluorescence, activation analysis and mass spectrometry. Gamma ray spectrometry is the only method which enables the simultaneous determination of U, Th and K. Further advantage is the easy sample preparation (pulverizing). The assumption of radioactive equilibrium within the U^{238} and Th^{232} series and of a constant K^{40}/K ratio is fulfilled in almost all rock types (Rybach, 1976; Rao *et al.*, 1976). The only limitation of this technique is its moderate sensitivity. A rock with e.g. 3 ppm U, 10 ppm Th and 2.5 percent K emits only 0.3γ quanta per sec and gram in the energy interval which is mainly used for measurements. Thus one has to deal with low radiation intensities since sample size and weight is usually limited to a few hundred grams. Due to this low intensity sensitive detectors like NaI (T1) must be used in combination with appropriate shielding against background radiation (Rybach, 1976). The detection limit with an equipment of this type is about 0.05 HGU. The gamma ray spectra are read out in digital form. Heat production varies over several orders of magnitude which reflects the geochemical conditions during rock formation: (i) During magmatic differentiation Uranium(U) and Thorium(Th) as well as Potassium(K) tend to be successively enriched in progressively more acidic phases; (ii) Sedimentary processes tend to fix the Th/U ratio depending upon the redox potential of the environment; (iii) Progressive metamorphism causes depletion of U and Th which then have a strong tendency to migrate towards regions with lower P/T conditions.

7.5 Relation of Heat Production to Other Geophysical Parameters

7.5.1 *Heat Production and Heat Flow*

Heier (1965) and Lambart and Heier (1968) have shown that processes of regional metamorphism, partial melting and magmatism which ceased long age in the Precambrian cratons, cause radioactive heat producing elements to migrate upwards and thereby increase their concentration at higher level in the crust.

Birch *et al.* (1968) and Lachenbruch (1968) established the linear relation between heat flow (Q) and radioactive heat generation (A_0) of the surface rocks in many regions older than Caledonian of the USA. This relation is expressed by,

$$Q = Q_0 + bA_0 \qquad \dots (7.2)$$

where, Q_0 and b are constants with dimension of heat flow and depth and are characteristic of large province of uniform tectonic structure. Q_0 is the intercept value of heat flow and b is the slope of the line relating Q and A_0.

The relation expressed by equation 7.2 has led to the division of the surface heat flow into two components: one is connected with a top radioactive layer and the other Q_0 (the reduced heat flow) conducted from the lower crust and mantle. This relation also provided the more clear idea for understanding of the vertical distribution of heat sources, our ability to calculate more reliable temperature depth profiles, and our ability to accurately map lateral variations of heat sources in the upper mantle (Roy *et al.*, 1972). Two vertical distributions of radioactivity have been proposed that are consistent with the observed linear relation between heat flow and heat generation (Birch *et al.*, 1968; Lachenbruch, 1968; Roy *et al.*, 1968): Model (1), a constant heat generation to the depth (step model) and Model (2), an exponentially decreasing with depth according to the relation,

$$A(Z) = A_0 e^{-Z/b} \qquad \dots (7.3)$$

Where 'Z' is depth, and $A_0 = A(Z = 0)$

The step model represents the simplest interpretation of the above relationship and it takes into account that the lateral variations of surface heat flow in a province are due to horizontal variation in a top radioactive layer of thickness 'b'. The layer subject to horizontal variation of heat production can be of any thickness for exponential model (Gupta and Sharma, 1979). The relationship between heat production and heat flow, whatever the model used to explain it, implies that beneath large intrusive bodies the whole crust has been affected and the original distribution of U and Th modified in some regular way (Rybach, 1976).

7.5.2 *Heat Production and Seismic Velocity*

Determination of heat production in rocks can be carried out on actual samples only. Thus direct information is limited to the uppermost few kilometers of the earth's crust from which surface samples, drill cores, etc., are available. To gain insight into the thermal regime of deeper regions heat production data of rocks in these zones must be evaluated from other evidence. Seismic velocity and its variation with depth can be measured by surface observations (Rybach, 1976). The variation of *Vp* in the crust reflects changes in rock type only (Birch, 1961); the same applies to the variation of heat production too. For practical purposes the empirical relationship found by Raybach and Cermak (1987) between heat production (*A*) and compressional wave velocity (*Vp*) is widely used. Using this relationship '*A*' values can be found from measured *Vp* values. For metamorphic rocks in which '*A*' also decreases with increasing *Vp*.

The depth dependence of radioactive heat production in the continental crust was investigated by converting seismic velocity profiles into heat production by means of an experimentally established relationship between heat production and compressional wave velocity (Cermak *et al.*, 1990). However, these two parameters are not likely to be related as velocity depends upon the major mineral constituents of rocks whereas heat production results from radiogenic components concentrated in both major and trace minerals in rocks (Fountain, 1986).

7.5.3 *Heat Production and Magnetic Properties*

The natural radiation level has been determined for the sediment samples of Ponnaiyar River, India. The average activity concentrations are within the world and Indian average values although some extreme values have been determined. The magnetic susceptibility measurement has been carried out to know the magnetization nature of the sediments. The mineralogical characterizations of the sediments have been carried out using Fourier Transform Infrared (FTIR) spectroscopic and XRD technique. The minerals such as quartz, microcline feldspar, orthoclase feldspar, kaolinite, calcite, gibbsite, montmorillonite, smectite, palygorskite and organic carbon are identified from FTIR analysis. Few minerals like zircon, monazite and hornblende are identified only in XRD analysis. Multivariate Statistical analyses were carried out between the parameters obtained from radioactivity analysis and other analyses to know the existing relations. The results suggested that the natural radioactivity level of the present sediments is mainly controlled by clay content and lesser extent to magnetic susceptibility (Suresh *et al.*, 2011).

7.6 Applications

7.6.1 *Radiometric Dating*

Radiometric dating (often called radioactive dating) is a technique used to date materials such as rocks, usually based on a comparison between the observed abundance of a naturally occurring radioactive isotope and its decay products, using known decay rates. It is the principal source of information about the absolute age of rocks and other geological features, including the age of the earth itself, and can be used to date a wide range of natural and man-made materials. Together with stratigraphic principles, radiometric dating methods are used in geochronology to establish the geological time scale. Among the best-known techniques are radiocarbon dating, potassium-argon dating and uranium-lead dating. By allowing the establishment of geological timescales, it provides a significant source of information about the ages of fossils and the deduced rates of evolutionary change. Radiometric dating is also used to date archaeological materials, including ancient artifacts (Sarkar *et al.*, 1995; Ray *et al.*, 2003; Sarangi *et al.*, 2004).

The most common sources of gamma rays are Potassium, Thorium, and Uranium. These are found in feldspar (granites, feldspathic), volcanic and igneous rocks, sand containing volcanic ash, and clays. The radioactive decay processes as given in Table 7.4 have proven particularly useful in radioactive dating for geological processes (Brown and Mussett 1993):

Table 7.4: The Radioactive Decay Processes

Parent	*Half-life (Billion yrs.)*	*Daughter*	*Materials Dated*
^{235}U	0.704	^{207}Pb	Zircon, uraninite, pitchblende
^{40}K	1.251	^{40}Ar	Muscovite, biotite, hornblende, volcanic rock, glauconite, K-feldspar
^{238}U	4.468	^{206}Pb	Zircon, uraninite, pitchblende
^{87}Rb	48.8	^{87}Sr	K- micas, K-feldspars, biotite, metamorphic rock, glauconite

The mathematical expression that relates radioactive decay to geologic time, is,

$$D = D_0 + N(e^{\lambda t} - 1) \qquad \ldots (7.4)$$

Where:

't' is age of the sample,

'D' is number of atoms of the daughter isotope in the sample,

'D_0' is number of atoms of the daughter isotope in the original composition,

'N' is number of atoms of the parent isotope in the sample at time 't' (the present), given by $N = N_o e^{-\lambda t}$, and

'λ' is the decay constant of the parent isotope, equal to the inverse of the radioactive half-life of the parent isotope times the natural logarithm of 2.

The above equation makes use of information on the composition of parent and daughter isotopes at the time the material being tested cooled below its closure temperature. This is well-established for most isotopic systems. However, construction of an isochron does not require information on the original compositions, using merely the present ratios of the parent and daughter isotopes to a standard isotope. Plotting an isochron is used to solve the age equation graphically and calculate the age of the sample and the original composition.

7.6.2 *Geothermal Structure of the Crust-Mantle*

Heat generation is not uniform within the crust. It is greatest in rocks of the granite family, in which the incompatible elements are most highly enriched. This means that the rate of heat generation is greatest in the upper part of the continental crust, where granites are most abundant, and decreases with depth, so that the 30°C km^{-1} geothermal gradient applies only to the upper crust. Oceanic crust, which is basaltic in composition, is even poorer in Uranium, Thorium, and Potassium; less heat is produced there, even than in the lower part of the continental crust. Once into the mantle, the geothermal gradient decreases again, because the mantle is even poorer in heat-producing isotopes.

Knowing the average heat production in the crust and surface heat flow, the temperature can be estimated in the crust-mantle using step model and exponential model related to heat production variation with depth (Birch *et al.*, 1968). The temperature (T) as a function of depth (Z) can be calculated considering step model (Gupta and Sharma, 1979, Gupta *et al.*, 1991; Sharma *et al.*, 2005):

$$T_z = T_0 + Q_i Z/k_i - A_i Z^2/2k_i \quad \ldots (7.5)$$

Where T_0 is the mean surface temperature, k_i and A_i are the thermal conductivity and radioactive heat production respectively in the rocks of the crust. Q_i is the heat flow at the top of ith layer.

Temperature-depth profile in the crust-mantle can be drawn considering exponential model (Lachenbruch and Sass, 1978) and using following equation (Gupta *et al.*, 1991):

$$T_z = T_0 + Q_r Z/k_1 + D^2 A_0 (1-e^{-Z/D})/k_1 \quad \ldots (7.6)$$

Where k_1 is the thermal conductivity of the crustal layer and 'Z' is the depth. Below the crust, if the mantle heat production is assumed negligible (Jones 1988), the temperature at depth 'Z' is given by:

$$T_z = T_{zm} + Q_r (Z-Zm)/k_2 \quad \ldots (7.7)$$

$Z > Zm$, where 'Zm' is the Moho depth and k_2 is the thermal conductivity of the upper mantle.

7.6.3 *Moho Heat Flow*

Estimation of the heat flow into the base of the crust, the mantle or Moho heat flow is not a straightforward task (Gupta *et al.*, 1991). Nevertheless, attempts often have been made to make a reasonable estimate. According to Roy *et al.* (1968, 1972) and Lachenbruch (1970), the reduced heat flow (Q_r) is the contribution from the deep crustal and/or mantle sources. However, on the basis of numerical stimulations of crustal models, Furlong and Chapman (1987) have inferred that 'Q_r' appears to be the mean heat flow at the characteristic depth '*D*', and that the general conclusion that 'Q_r' is an acceptable estimate for continental heat flow does not appear to be valid. Ashwal *et al.* (1987) have also indicated that lower crustal heat production would be represented in the reduced heat flow component, and the Moho heat flow could be significantly lower than the reduced heat flow (Gupta *et al.*, 1991; Kumar *et al.*, 2003; Kumar and Reddy, 2004).

7.7 Radioactive Studies in Deccan Trap

Deccan basalts have long been considered to be a product of Reunion plume—Indian lithosphere interaction, about 65 Ma ago. However, recent studies call into question their plume origin (Seth, 2005). Based on the heat flow and radioactive heat generation studies in southern Deccan Basalt Province (DBP), Kumar *et al.* (2007) suggested a radiogenic heat contribution of Deccan crust of ~38 mW m^{-2}, implying a Moho heat flow of ~7 mW m^{-2} and Moho temperature of ~280°C, which are similar to those in the adjoining Archaean Dharwar Craton. Therefore, it appears that there is no thermal trace of the supposed plume in the present-day crustal thermal regime of the southeastern Deccan basalt province.

References

1. Acton, G.D. and Gordon, R.G. (1989). "Limits on the age on the Deccan Traps of India from paleomagnetic and plate reconstruction data and their uncertainties", *J. Geophys. Res.,* V. 94, No. B12, pp. 17713–17720.
2. Aitken, M.J. (1974). "Physics and Archaeology", *Claren Press,* Oxford, p. 291.
3. Alagarsamy, R. (2009). "Environmental magnetism and application in the continental shelf sediments of India", *Marine Environmental Research*, V. 68(2), pp. 49–58.
4. Archie, G.E. (1942). "The electrical resistivity log as an aid in determining some reservoir characteristics", *Petroleum Transactions of AIME,* V. 146, pp. 54–62.
5. Aravamadhu, P.S. (1974). "Certain aspects of magnetic studies of charnockite at Waltair, India—Field investigations", *Canadian J. of Earth Sciences*, V. 11(4), pp. 503–509.
6. Ashwal, L.D., Morgan, P., Kelley, S.A. and Percival, J.A. (1987). "Heat production in an Archean crustal profile and implications for heat flow and mobilization of heat-producing elements", *Earth Planet. Sci. Lett.*, V. 85, pp. 439–450.
7. Athavale, R.N. (1970). "Paleomagnetism and Tectonics of Deccan Trap Lava Sequence at Amarkantak, India", *J. Geophys. Res.,* V. 75(20), pp. 4000–4006, doi: 10.1029/JB075i020p04000.
8. Basu, Sai bal (1990). "Clay mineralogy and pressure analysis from seismic information in Krishna-Godavari basin", *India Society of Exploration Geophysicists,* pp. 1447–1454.
9. Bayuk, Y.I. and Tedeyev, R.V. (1974). "The longitudinal wave velocity in rock samples under the simultaneous action

of high pressure and temperature Izvestiya", *Physics of the Solid Earth,* V. 10, pp. 521–526.

10. Beck, A.E. (1957). "A steady state method for the rapid measurement of the thermal conductivity of rocks", *J. Sc. Instrum,* V 34(5), pp. 186.
11. Beck, A.E. (1965). "Techniques of measuring heat flow on land, in Terrestrial Heat Flow", Geoph. Mon. Ser. No. 8: *Am. Geophys. Union,* pp. 24–50.
12. Behn, M.D. and Kelemen, P.B. (2003). "Relationship between seismic P-wave velocity and the composition of anhydrous igneous and metaigneous rocks", *Geochem. Geophys. Geosyst.,* V. 4(5), pp. 57, 1041.
13. Benfield, A.E. (1939). "Terrestrial heat flow in Great Britain", *Proceedings of the Royal Society of London,* A 173, pp. 428–50.
14. Besse, J. and Courtillot, V. (1991). "Revised and synthetic apparent polar wander paths of the African, Eurasian, North American and Indian plates, and true polar wander since 200Ma", *J. Geophys. Res.,* V. 96, pp. 4029–4050.
15. Birch, F. (1954). "The present state of geothermal investigations", *J. Geophysics, V 19 (4), Technical Papers,* p. 645.
16. Birch, F. (1960). "The velocity of compressional waves in rocks to 10 kilobars: 1", *J. Geophys. Res.,* V. 65, pp. 1083–1102.
17. Birch, F. (1961). "The velocity of compressional waves in rocks to 10 kilobars: 2", *J. Geophys. Res.,* V. 66, pp. 2199–2224.
18. Birch, F. (1966). "Thermal conductivity and diffusivity", Clark SP Jr. (ed.), Handbook of Physical Constants, rev. ed., Memoir 97, pp. 97–173, *Geol. Soc. America.*
19. Birch, F., Roy, R.F. and Decker, E.R. (1968). "Heat flow and thermal history in New York and New England, in Studies of Appalachian Geology: Northern and Maritime", edited by E. Zen, W.S. White, J.B. Hadley and J.B. Thompson, Jr. Interscience, New York, 475, pp. 437–451.

20. Black, P.R. and Braile, L.W. (1982). "Pn velocity and cooling of the continental lithosphere", J. Geophys. Res., V. 87, pp. 10, 557–10, 568.
21. Blackett, P.M.S. (1952). "A negative experiment relating to magnetism and the Earth's rotation", *Phil. Trans. R. Soc. Lon. A,* pp. 245, 309–370.
22. Bodmer, Rene, Ward, S.H. and Morrison, H.F. (1968). "On induced electrical polarization and ground-water", *J. Geophysics,* V 33, No. 5, pp. 805–821.
23. Bouguerra, A., Laurent, J.P., Goual, M.S. and Queneudec, M. (1997). "The measurement of the thermal conductivity of solid aggregates using the transient plane source technique", *J. Physics D: Applied Physics,* 30 pp. 2900–2904.
24. Brace, W.F. (1971). "Resistivity of saturated crustal rocks to 40 km based on laboratory studies", in the Structure and Physical Properties of the Earth's Crust, Geophys. Mono. Series, Vol. 14, J.G. Hancock, ed., AGU, Washington, pp. 243–256.
25. Bradley, R.S., Jamil, A.K. and Munro, D.C. (1964). "The electrical conductivity of olivine at high temperatures and pressures", Geochimica et. Cosmochimica Acta, V28, pp. 1669–1678, Bradley.
26. Bridgeman, P.W. (1949). "The high pressure behavior of miscellaneous minerals", *Am. J. Sci.,* V. 37, pp. 7–18.
27. Brigand, F., Chapman, D.S. and Le Douaran, S. (1990). "Thermal conductivity in sedimentary basins predicted from oil exploration well data", *Bull. Am. Assoc. Pet. Geol.,* V 74, pp. 1459–1477.
28. Brown, G.C. and Mussett, A.E. (1993). "The Inaccessible Earth. An Integrated View of its Structure and Composition", *2nd ed. London: Chapman and Hall.*
29. Caner, B. (1970). "Electrical conductivity structure in western Canada and petrological interpretation", *J. Geomag. Geoelect,* 22, pp. 113–129.
30. Carlslaw and Jaeger (1959). Carslaw, H.S. and Jaeger, J.C. (1959). "Conduction of Heat in Solids", Second ed.: Oxford, Oxford University Press, p. 510.

31. Carmichael, R.S. (1982). "Magnetic properties of minerals and rocks", in Carmichael, R.S., ed., Handbook of Physical Properties of Rocks, Vol. II: CRC Press, Boca Raton, Fla, 345 p.
32. Carey, S.W. (1958). "The tectonic approach to continental drift", in Carey, S.W. (ed.), Continental Drift, A Symposium, Geology Department, University of Tasmania, Hobart, pp. 177–356.
33. Castagna, J.P., Batzle, M.L. and Eastwood, R.L. (1985). "Relationships between compressional wave and shear-wave velocities in clastic silicate rocks to hydrocarbon exploration", *Am. Assn. Petr. Geol., Memoir 26, J. Geophysics,* 50(4), pp. 571–581.
34. Cathrine Fox Maule, Michael E. Purucker Nils Olsen and Klaus Mosegaard (2005). "Heat Flux Anomalies in Antarctica Revealed by Satellite Magnetic Data", Science, V. 309, No. 5733, pp. 464–467.
35. Cermak, V. and Rybach, L. (1982). "Thermal conductivity and specific heat of minerals and rocks", in Angenheister, G(Ed.) Physical properties of rocks, Landolt-Bormstrin new series, Vol. V(a) Springs, Berlin, Heidenberg, N.Y., pp. 305–343.
36. Cermak, V., Bodri, L. and Rybach, L. (1991). "Radioactive heat production in the continental crust and its depth dependence", in Terrestrial Heat Flow and the Lithosphere structure (Eds. Cermak, V and Rybach, L) Springer-Verlag, New York, pp. 23–69.
37. Cermak, V., Bodri, L., Rybach, L. and Buntebarth, G. (1990). "Relationship between seismic velocity and heat production: Comparison between two sets of data and test of validity", Earth Planet. Sci. Lett., 99, pp. 48–57.
38. Chinh, P.D. (2000). "Electrical properties of sedimentary rocks having interconnected water-saturated pore spaces", *J. Geophysics;* July–August 2000; V. 65; No. 4, pp. 1093–1097; 2000 *Society of Exploration Geophysicists.*

39. Choquette, P.W. and Pray, L.C. (1970). "Geologic nomenclature and classification of porosity in sedimentary carbonates", *Bull. Am. Assn. Petr. Geol.*, 54, No. 2, pp. 207–250.
40. Christensen, N.I. and Mooney, W.D. (1995). "Seismic velocity structure and composition of the continental crust: A global view", *J. Geophys. Res.*, 100, pp. 9761–9788.
41. Clark, Sydney P. Jr. (1966). "Thermal conductivity", Handbook of Physical Constants Am. Assn. Petr. Geol Mem., pp. 459–482.
42. Clauser, C. and Huenges, E. (1995). "Thermal conductivity of rocks and minerals, in Rock Physics and Phase Relations", A Handbook of Physical Constants, AGU Ref. Shelf, Vol. 3, edited by T.J. Ahrens, pp. 105–126, AGU, Washington, D.C.
43. Collinson, D.W. (1983). "Methods in Rock Magnetism and Palaeomagnetism, Techniques and Instrumentation", Chapman and Hall, London, p. 503.
44. Collinson, D.W. and Molyneux, L. (1967). "An instrument for the measurement of isotropic initial susceptibility of rock samples, Methods in Pleomagnetism", D.W. Collinson, K.M. Creer and S.K. Runkorn (Eds.), Elsevier, Amsterdom, 1967.
45. Cordell, B.M. (1980). "Martian climatic change—A magnetic trigger", *Geophysics. Res. Lett.*, V. 7, pp. 1065–1068.
46. Coster, H.P. (1948). "The electrical conductivity of rocks at high temperatures", *M.N.R.A.S. Geophys. Suppl.*, 5, pp. 193.
47. Cull, J.P. (1974). "Thermal conductivity probes for rapid measurements in rock", *J. Phys. E. Sci. Instrum.*, V. 7, pp. 771–774.
48. Cull, J.P. and Denham, D. (1979). "Regional variations in Australian Heat Flow", *B.M.R.J. Aust. Geol. Geophys*, 4, pp. 1–13.
49. Daily, W.D. and Dyal, P. (1979). "Theories for the origin of lunar magnetism Physics of the Earth and Planetary Interiors", V 20, Issues 2–4, pp. 255–270.
50. Devey, C.W. and Stephens, W.E. (1991). "Tholeciitic dykes in the Seychelles and the original spatial extent of the Deccan Traps", *J. Geol. Soc. London*, V 148, pp. 979–983.

51. Dortman, N.B. (1976). "Fizicheskiye svoystva gornykh porod ipoleznykh skopayemykh (petrofizika); spravochnik geofizika, Izdat Nedra", Moscow, USSR, 527.
52. Duba, A. (1972). "The electrical conductivity of olivine", *J. Geophys. Res.*, V 77, pp. 2483–2495.
53. Duba, A., Heard, H.C. and Snock, R.N. (1974). "Electrical conductivity of olivine at high pressure and under controlled oxygen fugacity", *Journal of Geophysical Research*, pp. 79, 1667–l 673.
54. Duffy, T.S. and Ahrens, T.J. (1992). "Sound velocities at high pressure and temperature and their geophysical implications", *J. Geophys. Res.*, 97, pp. 4503–4520.
55. Dullien, F.A.L. (1992). "Porous Media, Fluid Transport and Pore Structure", *2nd edition, Academic Press*, Ney York.
56. Dvorak, Z. (1973). "Electrical Conductivity of several samples of olivinites, peridotites and dunites as a function of pressure and temperature", *J. Geophysics*, 38, pp. 14–244.
57. Fielitz, K. (1971). "Elastic wave velocities in different rocks at high pressures and temperatures up to 750°C", *J. Geophysics*, 37, pp. 943.
58. Foster, R.J. (1971). "Physical geology", *Merrill (Columbus, Ohio),* VIII, p. 526.
59. Fountain, D.M. (1986). "Is there a relationship between seismic velocity and heat production for crustal rocks?" *Earth Planet. Sci. Lett.*, V. 79, Issues 1–2, pp. 145–150.
60. Furlong, K. and Chapman, D.S. (1987). "Crustal heterogeneities and the thermal structure of the continental crust", *Geophysics. Res. Lett.,* 105, pp. 27, 917–27.
61. Gebrande, H., Kern, H. and Rumel, F. (1982). "Elasticity and Inelasticity", Landolt-Bornstein Numerical data and functional relationship in Science and Technology (K.H. Hellwege, Ed), New Series: Group V, Geophysics and Space Research Vol. 1. Physical Properties of rocks Sub volume b, pp. 1–233. Springer Verlag, Berlin, Heidelberg, New York.
62. Gilbert, W. (1600). De Magnete, magnetisque corporibus, et de magnete tellure: Petrus Short", London, translated by

P, Fleury Mottelay in 1892, published in 1958 by Dover Publications, Mineola, NY, p. 368.

63. Gopal, B.V. and Sharma, S.R. (2011). "Thermal Diffusivity Measuring Apparatus with PC based Data Acquisition and Processing", *Jr. Instrumentation Society of India*, V 41(1), pp. 41–43.
64. Grasso, M., Lentini, F., Nairn, A.E.M. and Vigliotti, L. (1983). "A geological and paleomagnetic study ofthe Hyblean volcanic rocks", *Sicily, Tectonophysics*, pp. 98, 271–295.
65. Gupta, H.K., Rao, R.U.M., Srinivasan, R., Rao, G.V., Reddy, G.K., Dwivedy, K.K., Banerjee, D.C., Mohanty, R. and Satyasaradhi, Y.R. (1999). "Anatomy of surface rupture zones of two stable continental region earthquakes, 1967 Koyna and 1993 Latur, India", *Geophysics. Res. Lett.*, 26, pp. 1985–1988.
66. Gupta, M.L. (1960). "A rapid in-situ method for determining thermal conductivities", *J. Sci. Indust. Res.*, V 19B, pp. 240–243.
67. Gupta, M.L. and Venkateswar, Rao (1970). "Heat Flow studies under upper mantle Project", *Bull. of NGRI,* V 18 (3&4), pp. 87–104.
68. Gupta, M.L. and Sharma, S.R. (1979). "Crustal thermal structure of Dharwar Craton", Proc. 3rd Workshop on Status, Problems and Programmes in Indian Peninsular Shield, Hyderabad, pp. 284–296.
69. Gupta, M.L., Sharma, S.R. and Saxena, V.K. (1986). "Detection and delineation of areas of underground mine fires", *Proceedings of the seminar on 'Mine Climate', Sindri (Bihar),* July 1986, pp. 4–9.
70. Gupta, M.L., Sundar, A. and Sharma, S.R. (1991). "Heat flow and heat generation in the Archean Dharwar cratons and implications for the southern Indian Shield geotherm and lithospheric thickness", *Tectonophysics*, V. 194, pp. 107–122.
71. Gupta, M.L., Sharma, S.R., Drolia, R.K. and Singh, S.B. (1983). "Surface thermal conditions of Pugga Valley, Hydrothermal field, Himalaya, India", *J. Geophysics,* V. 54, pp. 51–59.

72. Gupta, M.L., Sharma, S.R., Sundar, A. and Singh, S.B. (1987). "Geothermal studies in the Hyderabad granitic region and the crustal thermal structure of the southern Indian Shield", Tectonophysics, V 140, pp. 257–264.
73. Gupta, M.L., Sundar, A., Sharma, S.R. and Singh, S.B. (1993). "Heat flow in the Bastar Craton, central Inrian Shield: Implications for thermal characteristics of Proterozoic cratons", *Phys. Earth Planet. Inter.*, V. 78, pp. 23–31.
74. Gupta, S.L. and Kumar, V. (1976). "Hand book of Electronics", Pragati *Prakashan, Meerut*, India, pp. 195–210.
75. Haack, U. (1982). "Radioactive Isotopes in Rocks, Landolt-Bornstein Numerical data and functional relationship in Science and Technology" (K.H. Hellwege, Ed), New Series: Group V. Geophysics and Space Research, Vol. 1, *Physical Properties of rocks.* Sub volume B, 1–233, Springer Verlag, Berlin, Heidelberg, New York.
76. Hall, J. and Simmons, G. (1979). "Seismic Velocities of Lewisian metamorphic rocks at 8 k bar Relationship in crustal layering in north Britain", *J. Geophys*, pp. 58, 337–58, 347.
77. Hearst, J.R. and Nelson, P.H. (1985). "Well logging for physical properties", Mc Graw Hills Book Co. N.Y., pp. 571.
78. Heier, K.S. (1965). "Radioactive Elements in the Continental Crust", *Nature,* 208, p. 479.
79. Henkel, H. (1976). "Studies of density and magnetic properties of rocks from Northern Sweden", *Pageoph, Birkhauser Verlag, Basel,* V. 114, pp. 235–249.
80. Horai, K. (1971). "Thermal conductivity of rock-forming minerals", *Journal of Geophysical Research*, V. 76, pp. 1278–1308.
81. Hughes, H. (1955). "The pressure effect on the electrical conductivity of Peridot", *J. Geophys. Res.*, V. 60, pp. 187–191.
82. Hunt, C.P., Moskowitz, B.M. and Banerjee, S.K. (1995). "Magnetic properties of rocks and minerals: in Rock Physics and Phase Relations", T.J. Ahrens, ed., AGU, Washington DC, pp. 189–204.

83. Hurley, P.M. and Fairbairn, H.W. (1953). "Radiation damage in zircons: A possible age method", *Bull. Geol. Soc. Am.*, 64, pp. 659–674.
84. Hyde, E.K. (1964). "The Nuclear Properties of the Heavy Elements III", *Prentice-Hall, Inc. Englewood Cliffs, New Jersey,* pp. 487–507.
85. Hyndman, R.D., Jaeger, J.C. and Sass, J.H. (1969). "Heat Flow measurements on the southwest coast of Australia", *Earth Planet. Sci. Lett.*, 7, pp. 12–16.
86. Irving, E. North, F.K. and Couillard, R. (1974). "Oil, Climate and Tectonics", *Canadian J. of Earth Sciences*, 11, pp. 1–17.
87. Irving, E. and Pullaih, G. (1976). "Reversals of geomagnetic field, magneto-stratigraphy and relative magnitude of Paleosecular variation in the Phanerozoic", *Earth Science Revs.,* V. 12, pp. 35–64.
88. Ito, K. and Tatsumi, Y. (1995). "Measurement of elastic wave velocities in granulite and amphibolite having identical H_2O-free bulk compositions up to850°C at 1 GPa", *Earth Planet. Sci. Lett.*, 1995, pp. 133, 255–264.
89. Iyer, H.M., Gaur, V.K., Rai, S.S., Ramesh, D.S., Rao, C.V.R., Srinagesh, L.D. and Suryaprakasam, K. (1989). "High velociy anomaly beneath the Deccan volcanic province: evidence from seismic tomography", *Proc. Indian Acad. Sci. (EPS),* V. 98, pp. 31–60.
90. Jason, Z. Han; Douglas, R. Schmitt; Daniel, Collis and Javier, Escartin (2004). "Laboratory determination of velocity anisotropy", *2004 CSEG National Convention.*
91. Jones, M.Q.W. (1988). "Heat Flow in the Witwatersrand basin and environs and its significance for south African shield geotherm and lithosphere thickness", *J. Geophys. Res.*, V 93, pp. 3243–3260.
92. Kaila, K.L., Chowdhury, K. Roy, Reddy, P.R., Krishna, V.G., Narain, H., S., Subbotin, I., Sollugub, V.B., Chekunov, A.V., Kharetchko, G.E., Lazarenko, M.A. and Ilchenko, T.V. (1979). "Crustal structure along Kavari–Udipi profile in the Indian peninsular shield from deep seismic soundings", *J. Indian Geol. Soc.*, V. 20, pp. 307–333.

93. Kaila, K.L. and Krishna, V.G. (1992). "Deep seismic sounding studies in India and major discoveries", *Current Science*, V. 62, pp. 117–154.
94. Kanamori, H., Fujii, N. and Mizutani, H. (1968). "The measurement of thermal diffusivity of rock forming minerals over the temperature range from 300°K to 1100°K", *J. Geophys. Res.*, 73, pp. 595–605.
95. Kappelmeyer, O. and Haenel, R. (1974). "Geothermics with special reference to application", Geoexploration Monographs Series 1, No. 4, Geo publication Associates, Berlin, pp. 51–59.
96. Karner, S.L., Marone, C. and Evans, B. (1997). "Laboratory studies of fault heating and Lithification in simulated fault gauge under hydrothermal conditions", *Tectonophysics*, 277, pp. 41–55.
97. Keller, G.V. (1966). "Electrical properties of rocks and minerals", S.P. Clark, Jr., Ed. Handbook of physical constants, *Am. Assn. Petr. Geol. Mem.*, 1997, pp. 553–577.
98. Kern, H. (1978). "The effect of high temperature and high confining pressure on compressional wave velocities in quart bearing and quartz free igneous and metamorphic rocks", *Tectonophysics*, 44, pp. 185–203.
99. Kern, H. (1982). "Elastic wave velocities and constants of elasticity of rocks at elevated pressures and temperatures", *Physical properties of rocks, V 9/b (Eds. Argenheister, G., Landolt-Bornstein,* N.Y., pp. 128–129.
100. Kern, H. and Richter, A. (1981). "Temperature derivatives of compressional and shear wave velocities in crustal and mantle rocks at 6 k bar confining pressure", *J. Geophys.*, 49, pp. 47–56.
101. Kern, H. and Tubia, J.M. (1993). "Pressure and temperature dependence of P- and S-wave velocities, seismic anisotropy and density of sheared rocks from the Sierra Alpujata massif (Ronda peridotites, Southern Spain)", *Earth Planet. Sci. Lett.*, V 119, Issues 1–2, pp. 191–205.
102. Khazanehdari, J., Rutter, E.H. and Brodie, K.H. (2000). "High-pressure-high-temperature seismic velocity structure of

the midcrustal and lower crustal rocks of the Ivrea-Verbano zone and Serie dei Laghi, NW Italy", *J. Geophys. Res.*, V. 105, No. B6, pp. 13, 843–858. High-pressure-high-temperature seismic velocity structure of the midcrustal and lower crustal rocks of the Ivrea-Verbano zone and Serie dei Laghi, NW Italy

103. Kim, Hyoung C. and Lee, Youngmin (2007). "Heat Flow in the Republic of Korea", *J. Geophys. Res.,* 112, B05413, doi:10.1029/2006JB004266
104. Kletetschka, G. and Stout, J.H. (1998). "The origin of magnetic anomalies in lower crustal rocks, Labrador", *Geophysics. Res. Lett.*, 25(2), pp. 199–202.
105. Knox, R.W.O'B. and Harland, R. (1979). "Stratigraphical relationships of the early Palaeogene ash-series of NW-Europe", *J. Geological Society, London,* 136, pp. 463–470.
106. Kozlovskaya, E., Janik, T., Yliniemi, J., Karatayev, G. and Grad, M. (2004). "Density-Velocity Relationship in the Upper Lithosphere obtained from P- and S-Wave Velocity Models along the Eurobridge'97 Seismic Profile and Gravity Data", *Acta Geophysica Polonica,* V. 52, No. 4, 2004.
107. Kubik, J. (1986). "Relation between the Heat Flow Field and distribution of Pn velocities for the European Contnent", *Stud. Geoph et Geod.*, 30, pp. 60–77.
108. Kubik, J. (1988). "The relationship between the field of surface heat flow and distribution of Pn wave velocities for the continents", *Stud. Geoph et Geod.*, 32, pp. 287–299.
109. Kumar, P.S. and Reddy, G.K. (2004). "Radioelements and heat production of an exposed Archaean crustal cross-section, Dharwar craton, south India", *Earth Planet. Sci. Lett.,* V 224, pp. 309–324.
110. Kumar, P.S., Basavalingu, B. and Srinivasan, R. (2003). "Origin of the Closepet Granite in the light of fabric, mineralogy and radioelemental composition", in Mohan, A., ed., Milestones in Petrology, Memoir 52, *Geological Society of India, Bangalore* (India), pp. 229–254.
111. Kumar P.S., Menon, R. and Reddy, G.K. (2007). "Crustal geotherms in southern Deccan Basalt Province, India: the

Moho is as cold as adjoining cratons", Foulger, G.R., Jurdy, D.M. (Eds), Plates, Plumes and Planetary Processes, *Geol. Soc. Am. Special paper,* Vol. 430, pp. 275–284.

112. Kwada, K. (1964). "Studies of the thermal state of the earth", 15, Variation of thermal conductivity of rocks, 1, *Bull Earthquake Res Institute, Tokyo Univ.*, 42, 631.
113. Kwada, K. (1966). "Variation of thermal conductivity of rocks", 2, *Bull Earthquake Res Institute, Tokyo Univ.*, 44, 1071.
114. Lachenbruch, A.H. (1968). "Geothermal models for Sierra Nevada", *J. Geophys. Res.*, V 73, pp. 6, 977–6, 989.
115. Lachenbruch, A.H. (1970). "Crustal temperatures and Heat production, Implications of the linear heat flow relation", *J. Geophys. Res.*, 75(17), pp. 3291–3300.
116. Lachenbruch, A.H. and Sass, J.H. (1978). "Models of an extending lithosphere and heat flow in the Basin and Range province" *Geol. Soc. Am.*, 152, 209–250.
117. Lagtovikowl, M. and Kropiek, V. (1976). "Changes of Electric Conductivity in the Neighbourhood in the Curie Temperature of Basalts", *Studia geoph, et geod,* 20, pp. 265–272.
118. Lambert, I.B. and Heier, K.S. (1968). "Estimates of the crustal abundances of thorium, uranium and potassium", *Chemical Geology*, V 3, Issue 4, pp. 233–238.
119. Lapointe, P., Chomyn, B.A., Morris, W.A. and Coles, R.L. (1984). "Significance of magnetic susceptibility measurements from the Lac Du Bonn Batholith, Manitoba, Canada", *Geoexploration*, V 22 (3–4), pp. 217–229.
120. Lastovickova, M. (1978). "Electrical resistivity of rocks in the heating and cooling cycle", *Stud. Geoph. et Geod.,* V 22, pp. 184–189.
121. Lin, W. and Wang, C.Y. (1980). "P-wave velocities in rocks at high pressure and temperature and the constitution of the central California crust", *Geophysical Journal of the Royal Astronomical Society,* V. 61, pp. 379–400.
122. Liu, Jian; Rixiang, Zhu; Zongshi, Ge and Shaoquan, Li (2003). "Magnetic properties and their paleoclimatic implications revealed from the last glacial eolian sedimentary sequence in

Pengze", Jiangxi. Science in China Series D: Earth Sciences, 2003, pp. 954–966.

123. Loper, D.E., Mc.Cartney, K. and Buzyna, G. (1988). "A model of correlated episodicity in magnetic field reversals, climate and mass extinctions", *J. Geol.*, V. 96, pp. 1–15.

124. Louzada, K.L., Weiss, B.P., Maloof, A.C., Stewart, S.T., Swanson-Hysell, N.L. and Soule, S.A. (2008). "Paleomagnetism of Lonar impact crator, India", *Earth Planet. Sci. Lett.,* V 275, pp. 308–319.

125. MacKay, M.E. Moore, G.F. Klaeschen, D. and Von Huene, R. (1995). "The case against porosity change: Seismic velocity decrease at the toe of the Oregon accretionary prism", *J. Geology;* V. 23, No. 9, pp. 827–830.

126. Mall, D.M. and Sharma, S.R. (2009). "Tectonics and thermal structure of western Satpura, India", Journal of Asian Earth Sciences, Vol. 34, Issue 3, pp. 450–457.

127. Manohar, R., Gupta, M. and Shukla, J.P. (2000). "Phase transition studies of some cholesteric liquid crystals and their mixtures using dielectric, optical transmittance and density measurement techniques", *J. Phy. Chem. Solid.,* V. 61, pp. 1465.

128. Marcela, L., Ramana, Y.V. and Gogte, B.S. (1987). "Electrical conductivity of some rocks from the Indian Subcontinent", *Studia. Geophy. ET Geod.,* V 31(1), pp. 60–72.

129. Mayhew, M.A. (1982). "Application of Satellite Magnetic Anomaly Data to Curie Isotherm Mapping", *J. Geophys. Res.*, V. 87, pp. 4846–4854.

130. Mayhew, M., LaBrecque, J. (1987). "Crustal geologic studies with Magsat and surface magnetic data", *Reviews of Geophysics*, V. 25, pp. 971–981.

131. Mishra, D.C. (1977). "Possible extension of the Narmada-Son lineament towards Murray ridge (Arabian Sea) and the eastern syn-taxial bend of the Himalayas", *Earth Planet. Sci. Lett.*, 36, pp. 301–308.

132. Mizutani, J. and Kanamori, H. (1967). "Electrical conductivities of rock forming minerals at high temperatures", *J. Physics of Earth*, 15, pp. 25–31.

133. Molyneux, L. (1971). "A complete result magnetometer for measuring the remanent magnetization of rocks", *Geophys. J. Astro. Soc.,* 24, pp. 429–433.
134. Mongelli, F. (1969). "Thermal conductivity measurement of some apulian limestones by the 'cut core', method", *Associa. Zone. Geofisica Italiana Napoli Ottobre:* 1–4.
135. Mostafa, M.S., Afify, N., Gaber, A. and Abozid, E.F. (2003). "Electrical Resistivity of Some Basalt and Granite Samples from Egypt", *Egypt. J. Sol.*, V. (26), No. (1), pp. 25–33.
136. Mukerji, T. and Mavk, Gary (1994). "Pore fluid effects on seismic velocity in anisotropic rocks", *J. Geophysics*, V. 59, No. 2, pp. 233–244, Doi. 10.1190/1.144358.
137. Mullins, C.E. (1977). "Magnetic susceptibility of the soil and its signiûcance in soil science—A review", *J. Soil Sci.,* V. 28, pp. 223–246.
138. Muxworthy, A.R., Schmidbauer, E. and Petersen, N. (2002). "Magnetic properties and Mössbauer spectra of urban atmospheric particulate matter: A case study from Munich, Germany", *Geophys. J. Int.* 2002, V. 150, pp. 558–570.
139. Negi, J.G., Agarwal, P.K. and Pandey, O.P. (1987). "Large variation of Curie Depth and Lithospheric thickness beneath the Indian subcontinent and a case for Magneto-thermometry", *Geophysical Journal of the Royal Astronomical Society*, 88, pp. 763–775.
140. Nelson, R.A. (1985). "Geologic analysis of naturally Fractured Reservoirs", *Gulf Publishing, Housten.*
141. Noritomi, K. (1961). "The electrical conductivity of rocks and the determination of electrical conductivity of the earth's interior", *J. Min. Coll. Akita Univ. Ser. AI,* pp. 27–59.
142. Norton, I.O. and Sclater, J.G. (1979). "A model for the evolution of the Indian Ocean and the break-up of Gondwanaland", *J. Geophys. Res.*, 84, pp. 6803–6830.
143. Petersen, N. and Bleil, U. (1982). "Magnetic properties, Landolt-Börnstein Numerical Data and Functional Relationships in Science and Technology" (K.H. Hellwege, ed.), New Series; Group V. Geophysics and Space Research,

Vol. 1 Physical Properties of Rocks, Subvolume b, 308–432. Springer-Verlag Berlin. Heidelberg, New York.

144. Phillips, D., Eberhart, Han, D.H. and Zoback, M.D. (1989). "Empirical relationships among seismic velocity, effective pressure, porosity and clay content in sandstone", *J. Geophysics,* January 1989; V. 54; No. 1, pp. 82–89, DOI: 10.1190/1.1442580.
145. Piper, J.D.A. (1987). "Paleomagnetism and the continental crust", *Halsted Press, John Wileye and Sons,* New York., pp. 19–30.
146. Rajendran, V.; Kumaran, S. Muthu; Jayakumar, T., Palanichamy, P. and Raj, Baldev (2002). "Measurement of Ultrasonic Velocity and Attenuation at Elevated Temperatures", NDE 2002 Predict. Assure. Improve, National Seminar of ISNT Chennai, Dec. 5–7, 2002.
147. Ramachandran, C. (1992). "P-wave velocity in granulites from South India: Implications for the continental crust", *J. Geophysics,* V 201, pp. 187–198.
148. Ramachandran, C. and Bosu, L.R. (1991). "Densities of high grade metamorphic rocks from south Indian granulite terrain", *Jour. Geol. Soc. India,* V. 37, pp. 287–293.
149. Ramananantoandro, R. and Manghnani, M.H. (1978). "Temperature dependence of the compressional wave velocity in an anisotropic dunite: Measurements to 500°C at 10 kbar", *Tectonophysics,* 47, pp. 73–84.
150. Rao, R.U.M., Rao, G.V. and Narain, Hari (1976). "Radioactive heat generation and heat flow in the Indian shield", *EPSL,* 30, pp. 57–64.
151. Rao, G.V.S. Poornachandra, Bhalla, M.S. (1984). "Lonar Lake: palaeomagnetic evidence of shock origin", *Geophysical Journal of the Royal Astronomical Society,* 77, pp. 847–862.
152. Rao, G.V.S., Poornachandra Mallikharjuna Rao, J. and Jaya Prasanna Lakshmi, K. (2000). "Alkali igneous rock of Deccan Traps from North west India and their palaeomagnetism", *Proc. Ind. Geol. Con., Dept. of Geo., M.L.S. University, Udaipur.*
153. Rao, G.V.S. Poornachandra, Rao, J., Mallikharjuna (2007). "Palaeomagnetic evidence for possible occurrence of

hydrocarbon in the Proterozoic Vindhyan Basin in India", *J. Applied Geochemistry*, V 9(1), pp. 105–111.

154. Rao, V. Vijaya and Tewari, H.C. (2008). "Deep Crustal Seismic Studies over the Indian Shield", *Deep Crustal Seismic Studies over the Indian Shield*, pp. 137–143.
155. Ray, J.S., Veizer, J. and Davis, W.J. (2003). "C, O, Sr and Pbisotope systematics of carbonate sequences of the Vindhyan Supergroup, India: Age, diagenesis, correlations and implications for global events", *Precamb. Res.*, V. 121, pp. 103–140.
156. Ray Labani, A. Bhattacharya and Roy, S. (2007). "Thermal Conductivity of Higher Himalayan Crystallines from Garhwal Himalaya, India", Tectonophysics, 434, pp. 71–79.
157. *Robert P.* 1988, "Electrical and Magnetic Properties of Materials", *Artech House, Inc., Norwood*, pp. 289–378.
158. Roy, R.F., Blackwell, D.D. and Decker, E.R. (1972). "Continental Heat Flow", Chapter 19, The nature of solid earth, E.C. Robertson (Ed.), Mc Graw Hill, N.Y., pp. 506–544.
159. Roy, R.F., Blakwell, D.D. and Birch, F. (1968). "Heat generation of plutonic rocks and continental heat flow provinces", *EPSL*, 5, pp. 1–12.
160. Roy, S. and Rao, R.U.M. (2000). "Heat flow in the Indian shield", *J. Geophys. Res.*, 105, 25, 587–25, 604.
161. Ray, J.S., Veizer, J. and Davis, W.J. (2003). "C, O, Sr and Pb isotope systematics of carbonate sequences of the Vindhyan Supergroup, India: age, diagenesis, correlations and implications for global events", *Precamb. Res.*, V. 121, pp. 103–140.
162. Rybach, L. (1976). "Radioactive heat production in rocks and its relation to other petrophysical parameters", Pure and Applied Geophysics, 114, pp. 309–31.
163. Rybach, L. and Cermak, V. (1982). "Radioactive heat generation in rocks; Properties of rocks" (ed.) H.G. Angenheister. (Springer-Verlag) 1a, pp. 353–371.

164. Rybach, L. and Buntebarth, G. (1984). "The variation of heat generation, density and seismic velocity with rock type in the continental lithosphere", *Tectonophysics,* 103, pp. 335–344.
165. Rybach, L. and Cermak, V. (1987). "The depth dependence of heat production in the continental Lithosphere derived from Seismic Velocities", *Geophys. Res. Lett.,* 14, pp 311–313.
166. Sarangi, S., Gopalan, K. and Kumar, S. (2004). "Pb-Pb age of earliest megascopic, eukaryotic alga bearing Rohtas Formation, Vindhyan Supergroup, India: Implications for Precambrian atmospheric oxygen evolution", *Precamb. Res.,* V. 132, pp. 107–121.
167. Sarkar, A., Paul, D.K. and Potts, P.J. (1995). "Geochronology and geochemistry of the mid-Archean trondjemitic gneisses from the Bundelkhand craton, central India", in: Saha, A.K. (Ed.), *Recent Researches in Geology and Geophysics of the Precambrian, Recent Researches in Geology*, V. 16, pp. 76–92.
168. Sato, H., Sacks, S., Murase, T., Muncill, G. and Fukuyama, H. (1988). Attenuation of compressional waves in peridotite measured as a function of temperature at 200 Mpa, PAGEOPH, 128(1&2), pp. 433–447.
169. Scarlato, P., Poe, B.T., Freda, C. and Gaeta, M. (2004). "High-pressure and high-temperature measurements of electrical conductivity in basaltic rocks from Mount Etna, Sicily, Italy", *J. Geophys. Res.*, 109, B02210, doi:10.1029/2003JB002666.
170. Schober, M. (1971). "The electrical conductivity of some samples of natural olivine at high temperatures and pressures", *J. Geophysics,* 37, pp 283–292.
171. Schön, J.H. (1996). "Physical Properties of Rocks, Fundamentals and Principles of Petrophysics", *Handbook of Geophysical Exploration, Seismic Exploration*, Vol. 18, Elsevier.
172. Schult, A. (1970). "Effect of pressure on Curie temperature of titanomagnetites [$(1\text{-}x)\cdot Fe_3O_4 - x\cdot TiFe_2O_4$]", *Earth Planet. Sci. Lett.,* V 10, Issue 1, pp. 81–86.
173. Sheth, H.C. (2005). "From Deccan to Reunion: no trace of a mantle plume, Foulger", G. R., Natland, J.H., Presnall, D.C. anderson, D.L. (Editors), 'Plates, Plumes and Paradigms'.

Geological Society of America Special Paper 388, Chapter 29, pp. 477–501.

174. Sharma, S.R. (1982). "Thermo-physical and Electrical Properties of rocks under various temperature conditions", Ph.D. Thesis, Meerut University, India.
175. Sharma, S.R., Saxena, V.K., Sukhija, B.S. and Gupta, M.L. (1982). "Geothermal, geochemical and tritium investigations in Garampani hot spring area, N.C. Hills, Assam", *Geophys. Res. Bull.,* V. 20(4), pp. 205–212.
176. Sharma, S.R. (1987). "Laboratory measurements of resistivity of rocks—an aid for the interpretation of field resistivity data", *Geophys. Res. Bull.*, V 25(1), pp. 7–12.
177. Sharma, S.R. and Gupta, M.L. (1978). "Shallow thermal surveys in Tural, Rajwadi and Unhavare (Khed) hot spring areas, Konkan coast, India", *Geophys. Res. Bull.*, V. 16(2), pp. 111–120.
178. Sharma, S.R. and Veeraswami, K. (1998). "Temperature distribution in upper mantle beneath Hyderabad using long period EM and laboratory conductivity measurements", *IGU 35th Annual meeting, India,* p. 65.
179. Sharma, S.R., Gupta, M.L. and Mahesh, P.S. (1987). "Electrical conductivity of rocks at elevated temperatures and the electrical conductivity model of the earth's crust of the Indian Shield", *Proc. Seminar on Crustal Dynamics*, Jan. 22–23, 1986, IGU, Hyderabad, India, pp. 99–106.
180. Sharma, S.R., Sundar, A., Rao, V.K. and Ramana, D.V. (1991). "Surface heat flow and Pn velocity distribution in Peninsular India", *J. Geodynamics*, V13, Issue 1, pp. 67–76.
181. Sharma, S.R., Rao, G.V.S.P., Kaladhar Rao, K.P.C. and Srinivasa Rao, B. (2004). "Physical Properties of Deccan Basalts from Latur Area, Maharastra, India", *Indian Geophysical Union annual convention,* 29–31 Dec, Hyderabad, India, pp. 31.
182. Sharma, S.R., Rao, V.K., Mall, D.M. and Gaud, T.N. (2005). "Geothermal structure in a seismoactive Region of central India", *PAGEOPH,* V. 162, pp. 129–144.

183. Sharma, S.R., Poornachandra Rao, G.V.S. and Rao, V.K. (2006). "Heat Flow, Curie Depth and Composition of Lower Crust Beneath the Indian Shield", Advances in Geosciences, V.1., SE (Eds. Wing-HuenIp and Yen-Tai Chen), World Scientific Publishing Co. Pvt. Ltd., Singapore, pp. 189–195.
184. Shive, P.N., Blakely, R.J., Frost, B.R. and Fountain, D.M. (1992). "Magnetic properties of lower continental crust, Continental lower crust, Developments in Tectonics", D.M. Fountain, R. Arculus and R.W. Kay (Eds.), V 23, Elsevier, N.Y. pp. 145–177.
185. Shuey, R.T., Schellinger, D.K., Tripp, A.C. and Alley, L.G. (1977). "Curie depth determination from Aeromagnetic spectra", *Geophysical Journal of the Royal Astronomical Society,* 50, pp. 75–101.
186. Simmons. G. (1965). "Ultrasonics in geology" Proc. Inst. Electr. and Electron. Eng., V 53, pp. 1337–1345.
187. Simov, S.D. (1989). "Uranium deposits in the foothilis of a granite massif in the southeastern Alps", *IAEA Uranium deposits in metamorphic rocks,* Vienna.
188. Spencer, J.W. and Nur, A. (1976). "The effect of pressure, temperature and pore water on velocities in Westerly granite", *J. Geophys. Res.*, 81, pp. 899–904.
189. Steward, R. and Peselnick, L. (1977). "Velocity of compresional waves in dry Franciscan rocks to 8 kilobars and 300°C", *J. Geophys. Res.,* 82, pp. 2027–2039.
190. Stiller, H., Vollstadt, H., Seipold, U. and Wasch, R. (1976). "Electrical and thermal investigations of rocks and minerals under extreme P. and T. conditions", *Pure. Appl. Geophys.,* 114, pp. 263–272.
191. Subrahmanyam, C. and Verma, R.K. (1981). "Densities and magnetic susceptibilities of Precambrian rocks of different metamorphic grade (Southern Indian shield)", *J. Geophysics,* V. 49, pp. 101–107.
192. Sundar, A., Gupta, M.L. and Sharma, S.R. (1990). "Heat flow in the Trans-Aravalli igneous suite, Tusham, India", *J. Geodynamics,* V. 12(1), pp. 89–100.

193. Surma, F. and Geraud, Y. (2003). "Porosity and thermal conductivity of the Soultzsous Forêts Granite", *Pure. Appl. Geophys.,* 160, pp. 1125–1136.
194. Suresh, G., Ramasamy, V., Meenakshisundaram, V., Venkatachalapathy, R. and Ponnusamy, V. (2011). "A relationship between the natural radioactivity and mineralogical composition of the Ponnaiyar river sediments, India", *J. Environ. Radioact.,* 102(4), pp. 370–377.
195. Tarkov, A.P. and Vavakin, V.V. (1982). "Poisson's ratio behavior in various crystalline rocks: Application to the study of the Earth's interior", *Phys. Earth Planet. Inter.*, 29, pp. 24–29.
196. Tarling, D.H. (1983). "Paleomgnetism: Principles and applications in Geology, Geophysics and Archeology", *Chapman and Hall, London*, p. 379.
197. Telford, W.M., Geldart, L.P. and Sheriff, R.E. (1990). "Applied geophysics", Cambridge University Press.
198. Theilen, F. and Meissner, R. (1979). "A comparasion of crustal and upper mantle features in Fennoscandia and the Rhenish shield., two areas of recent uplift", *Tectonophysics*, 61, pp. 227–242.
199. Toft, P.B. and Haggerty, S.B. (1988). "Limiting depth of magnetization in cratonic lithosphere", *Geophysics. Res. Lett.*, 15, pp. 530–533.
200. Turner, S. and Tarling, D. (1982). "The lodont and other agnathan distributions as tests of Lower Palaeozoic continental reconstructions", *Palaeogeography, Palaeoclimatology, Palaeoecology,* 39, pp. 295–311.
201. Ursin, B. and Carcione, J.M. (2007). "Seismic-Velocity/Electrical-Conductivity Relations", *EGM 2007 International Workshop Innovation in EM, Grav and Mag Methods: A new Perspective for Exploration Capri,* Italy, April 15–18, 2007.
202. Uyeda, S. and Rikitake, T. (1970). "Terrestrial heat flow and electrical conductivity anomaly", *J. Geomag. Geoelect.*, 22, pp. 75–90.
203. Vandamme, D. and Courtillot, V. (1992). "Paleomagnetic constraints on the structure of the Deccan traps", *PEPI,* 74, pp. 241–261.

204. Vandamme, D., Courtillot, V. and Besse, J. (1991). "Palaeomagnetism and age determinations of the Deccan Traps (India): Results of a Nagpur-Bombay traverse and review of earlier work", *Rev. Geophys.,* 29, pp. 159–190.

205. Varaprasada Rao, S.M., Satyanarayana Murty, B.V. and Bhimasankaram, V.L.S. (1978). "Petro-physical properties (Density and magnetic-susceptibility) and lithological composition of some dolerite dykes of Andhra Pradesh, India", *J. Geophysics,* V. 44, pp. 353–356.

206. Verosub, K.L. and Banerjee, S.K. (1977). "Geomagnetic excursions and their paleomagnetic record 2", *Rev. Geophys.,* 15, 2, pp. 145–155.

207. Verosub, K.L. (1979). "Paleomagnetism of varved sediments from western New England: Secular variation", *Geophysics. Res. Lett.,* V. 6, pp. 245–248.

208. Von Herzen, R.P. and Maxwell, A.E. (1959). "The measurement of thermal conductivity of deep sea sediments by a Needle Probe Method, *J. Geophys. Res.,* 64, pp. 1550–1563.

209. Vorobyev, A.A., Zavodovskaya, Ye. K. and Salvikov, V.N. (1975). Variation of Electrical conductivity and radio emission of rocks and minerals during process attendant to heating", Dokl. Akad. Nank. *SSSR,* 220, pp. 1–3.

210. Wang, C.Y., Manga, M., Dreger, D. and Wong, A. (2004). "Stream flow increase due to rupturing of hydrothermal reservoirs: Evidence from the 2003 San Simeon, California, earthquake", *Geophysics. Res. Lett.,* 31, L10502, doi: 10.1029/2004GL020124.

211. Wang, Z. and Nur, A. (1992). "Aspects of Rock physics in Seismic Reservoir Surveillance", Reservoir Geophysics, Edited by Robert E. Sheriff, SEG, Tulsa, Oklahoma.

212. Waples, D.W. and J.S. Waples (2004). "A review and evaluation of specific heat capacities of rocks, minerals and subsurface fluids", *Part 1: Mineralsand nonporous rocks, Nat. Resour. Res.,* V. 13, pp. 97–122.

213. Wang Doujun; Li Heping; Yi Li; Zhang Weigang; Liu Congqiang; Suo Gengli and Ding, Dongye (2002). "The

electrical conductivity of gabbro at high temperature and high pressure", *Chinese J. Geochemistry*, V. 21, No. 3, pp. 252–257.

214. Wasilewski, P.J. and Mayhew, M.A. (1992). "The Moho as a magnetic boundary revisited", *Geophysics. Res. Lett.*, 19, pp. 2259–2262.
215. Watenbe, H. (1970). "Measurements of Electrical Conductivity of basalts at temperatures up to 1500°C and pressure to about 20 k bars, Special contributions", *Geophysics. Inst. Kyoto Univ.*, No. 10, pp. 159–170.
216. Whittaker, A., Chadwick, R.A. and Penn, I.E. (1986). "Deep crustal traverse across southern Britain from seismic reflection profiles", *Bulletin de la Societé Geologique de France,* 8, pp. 55–68.
217. Wohlenberg, J. (1982). "Density of rocks", K.H. Hellwege (ed.), Landolt-Börnstein, Group V.: *J. Geophysics,* Vol. 1: Physical Properties of Rocks, Sub Vol. A, Springer, Berlin, pp. 113–120.
218. Wollin, G., Ericson, D.B., Rayan, W.S.B. and Foster, J.H. (1971). "Magnetism of the earth and climate changes", *Earth Planet. Sci. Lett.*, 12, pp. 175–183.
219. Wyllie, M.R., Gregory, A.R. and Gardner, L.W. (1956). "Elastic wave velocities in heterogeneous and porous media", *J. Geophysics,* 21, pp. 41–70.
220. Zabloki, C.J. (1964). "Electrical Properties of Serpentinite from Mayaguez, Puerto Rico", in C.A. Burk (Ed) A Study of Serpentinite. *Natl. Acad. Sci. Natl. Res. Council, Washington, D.C.*, 1188, pp. 107–117.
221. Zamora, M., Sartoris, G. and Chelini, W. (1994). "Laboratory measurements of ultrasonic wave velocities in rocks from the Campi Flegrei volcanic system and their relation to other field data", *J. Geophys. Res.*, 99(B7), pp. 13553–13561.
222. Zoth, G. and Ha¨nel, R. (1988). Appendix in Ha¨nel, R., Rybach, L., Stegena, L. (Eds.), "Handbook of Terrestrial Heat-Flow Density Determination", *Kluwer Academic Publishers, Dordrecht,* pp. 449–466.